EASY PIANO

MODERN MOVIE
FAVORITES

T0088299

ISBN 978-1-4950-9928-1

HAL•LEONARD®

7777 W. BLUEMOUND RD. P.O. BOX 13819 MILWAUKEE, WI 53213

ALICE

from ALICE IN WONDERLAND - A Film by Tim Burton

Words and Music by
AVRIL LAVIGNE

Moderately fast

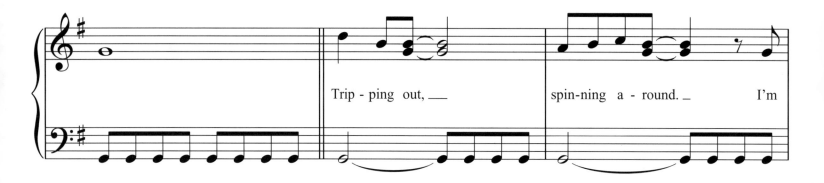

Trip - ping out, ___ spin-ning a - round. ___ I'm

un - der ground; ___ I ___ fell down, ___ yeah,

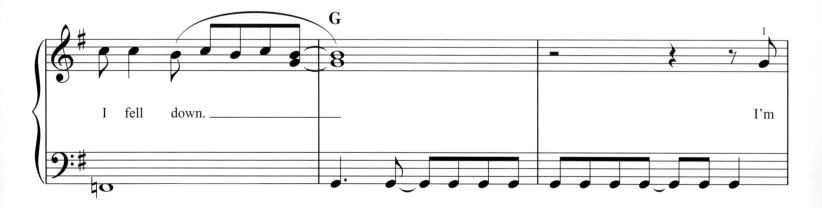

I fell down. ___ I'm

freak - ing out, ___ where am I now? ___ Up - side down, and I ___

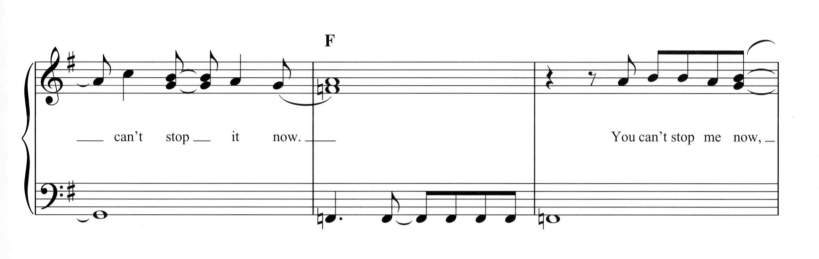

___ can't stop ___ it now. ___ You can't stop me now, ___

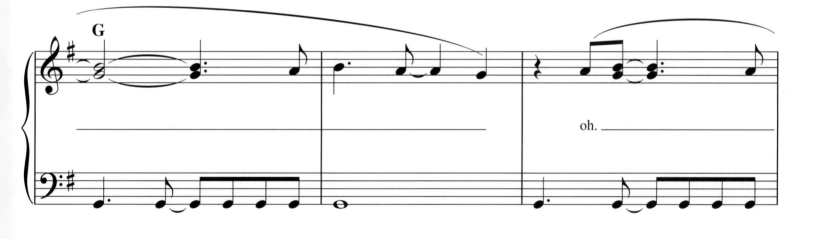

oh. ___

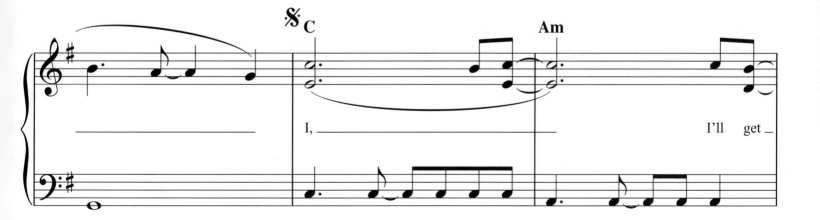

___ I, ___ I'll get ___

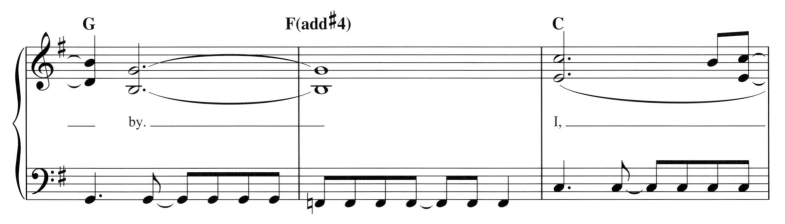

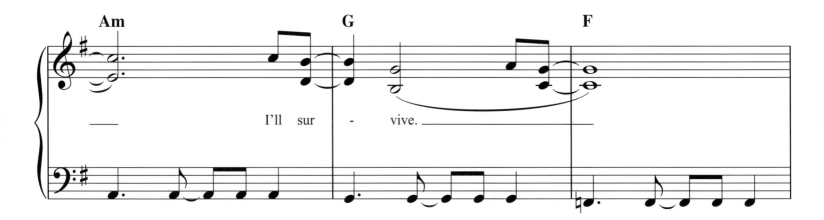

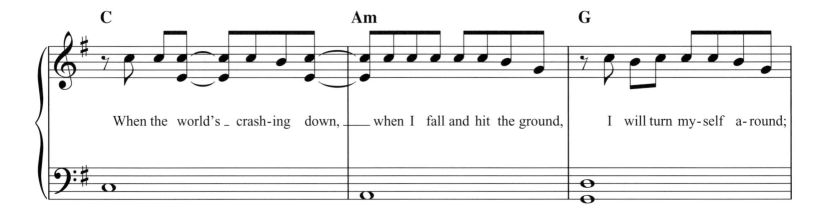

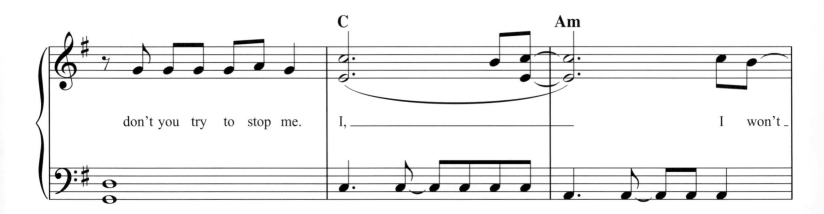

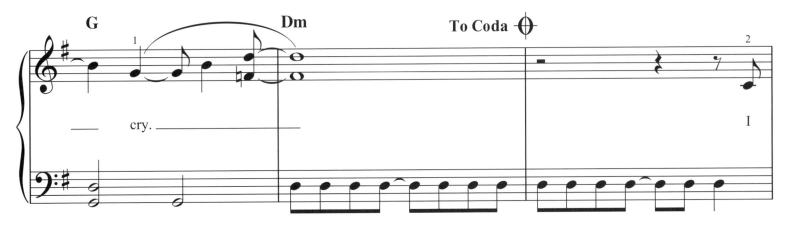

cry. I

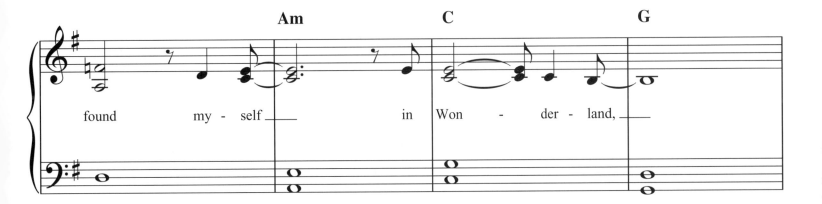

found my - self in Won - der - land,

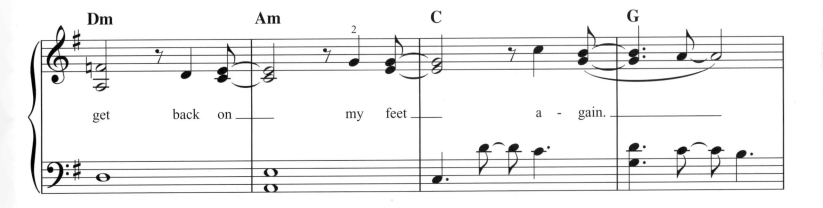

get back on my feet a - gain.

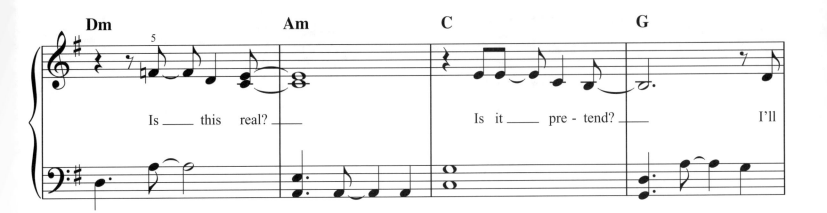

Is this real? Is it pre - tend? I'll

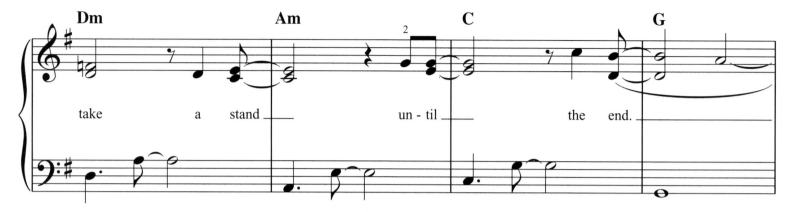

Dm   Am   C   G

take   a   stand ____   un - til ____   the   end. ____

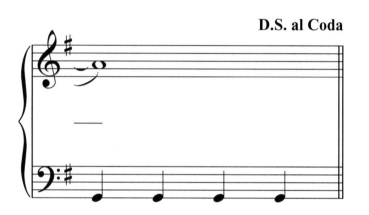

D.S. al Coda

CODA

C

I, ____

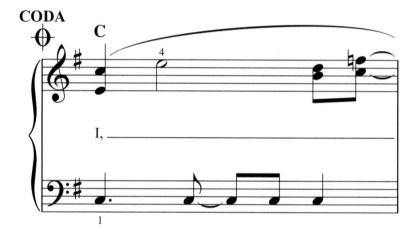

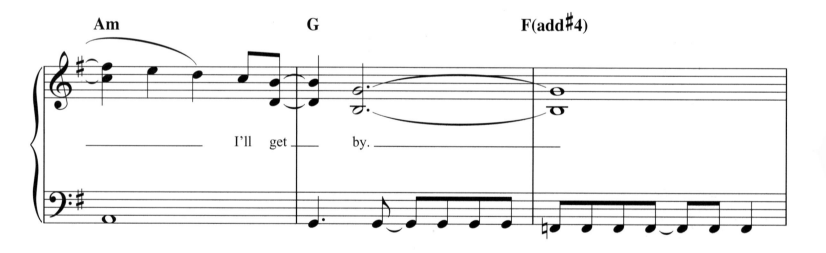

Am   G   F(add♯4)

____ I'll   get ____   by. ____

C   Am   G

I, ____   I'll   sur - vive. ____

When the world's — crash-ing down, —— when I fall and hit the ground,

I will turn my-self a-round; don't you try to stop me. I, ———————

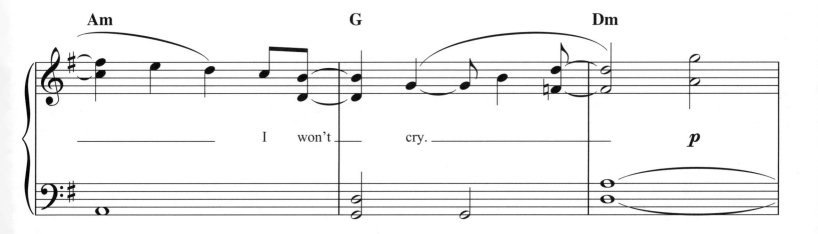

————————— I won't — cry. ———————— *p*

THE BARE NECESSITIES

from THE JUNGLE BOOK

Words and Music by
TERRY GILKYSON

Brightly

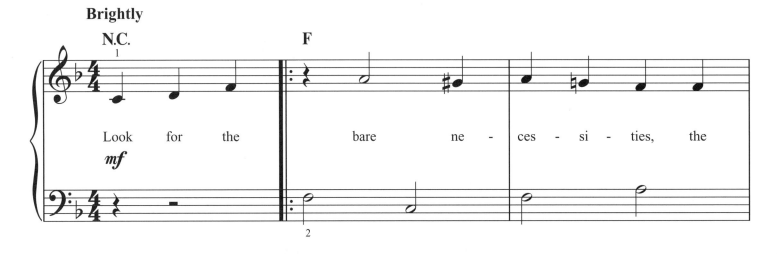

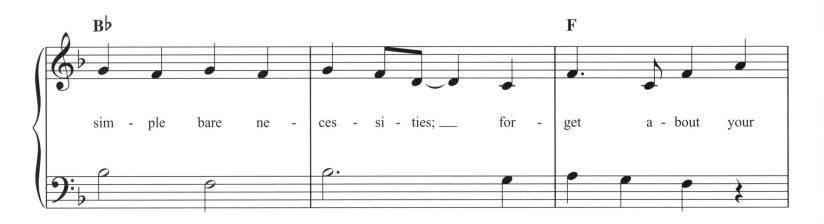

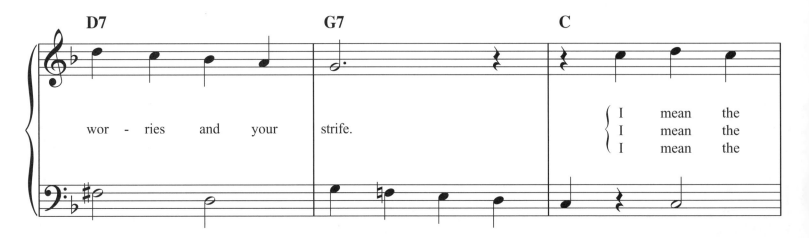

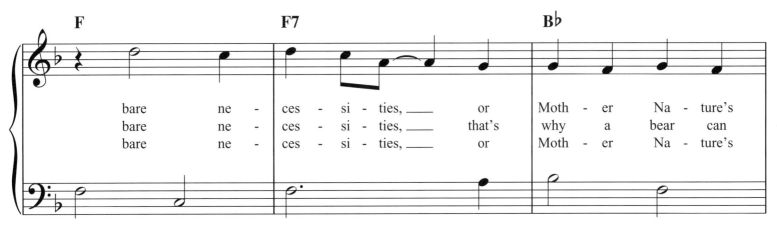

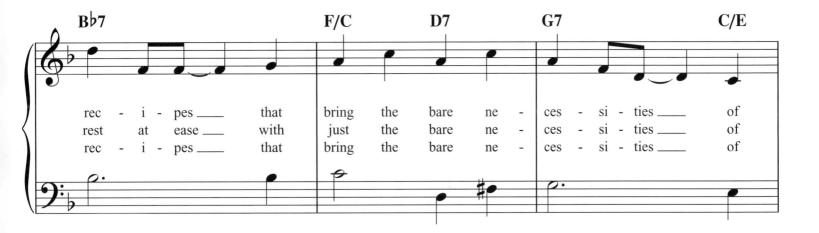

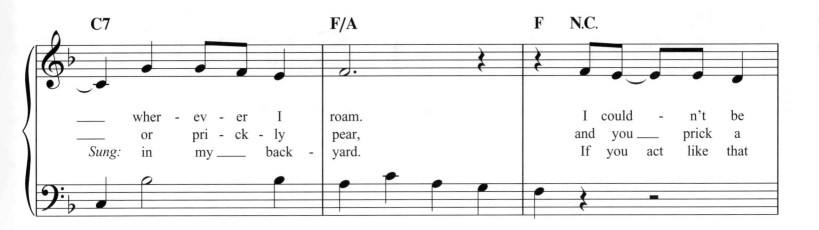

12

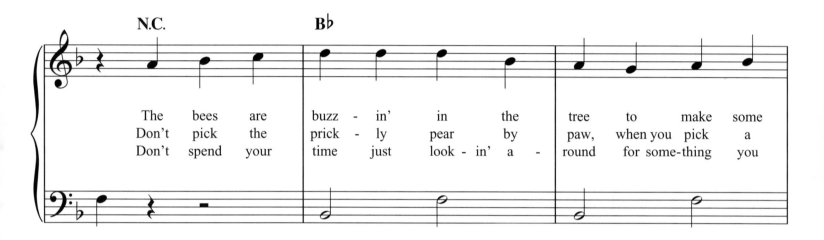

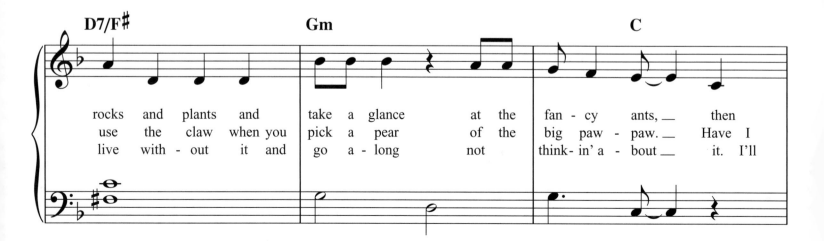

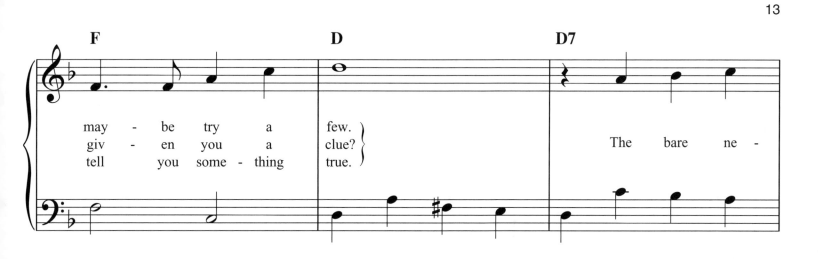

may - be try a few.
giv - en you a clue?
tell you some - thing true.

The bare ne -

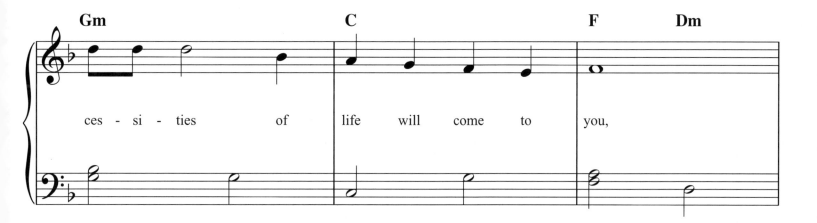

ces - si - ties of life will come to you,

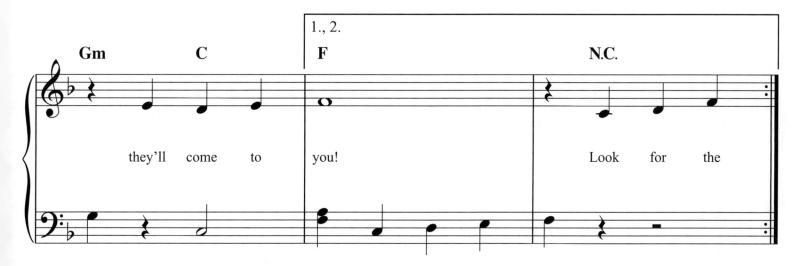

1., 2.

they'll come to you!

Look for the

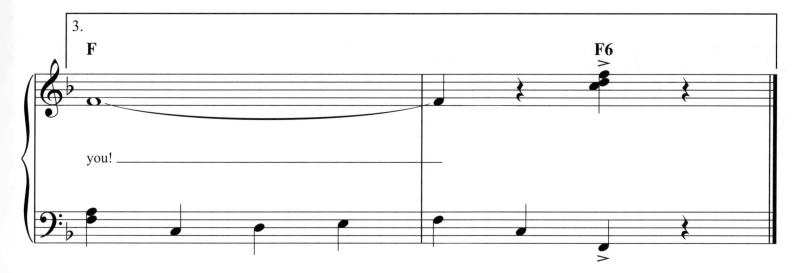

3.

you! _____

CAN'T STOP THE FEELING
from TROLLS

Words and Music by JUSTIN TIMBERLAKE,
MAX MARTIN and SHELLBACK

Moderate Funk groove

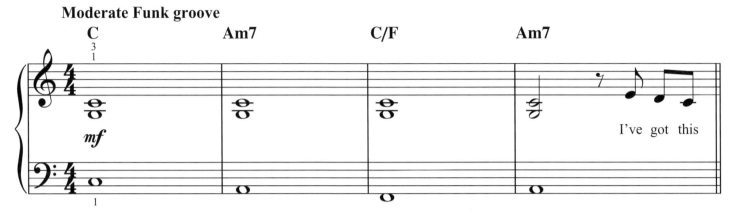

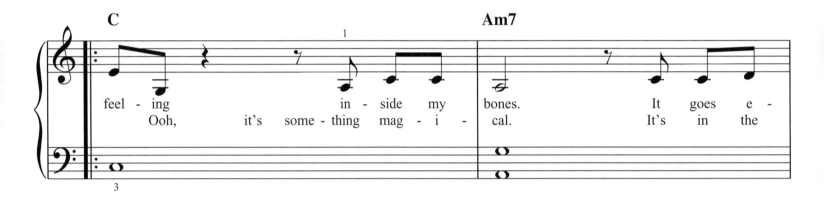

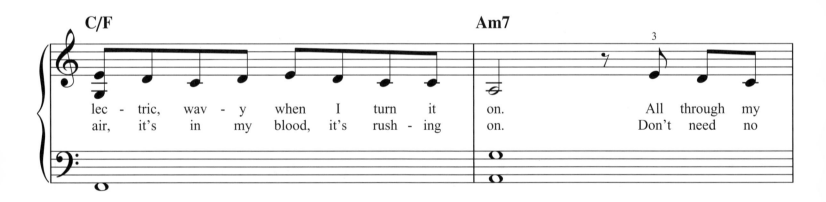

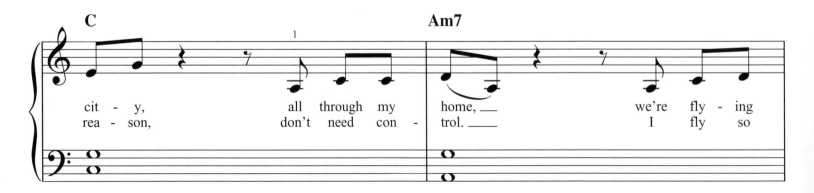

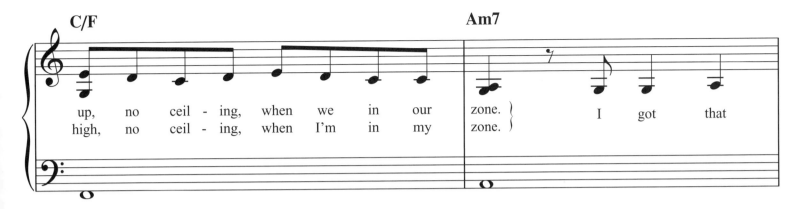

up, no ceil - ing, when we in our zone.
high, no ceil - ing, when I'm in my zone.
I got that

sun-shine in my pock-et, got that good soul in my feet. I feel that hot blood in my bod-y when it

drops, ooh. I can't take my eyes up off it, mov-ing so phe-nom - e-nal-ly. Room on

lock the way we rock it, so don't stop. Un - der the lights when ev - 'ry-thing

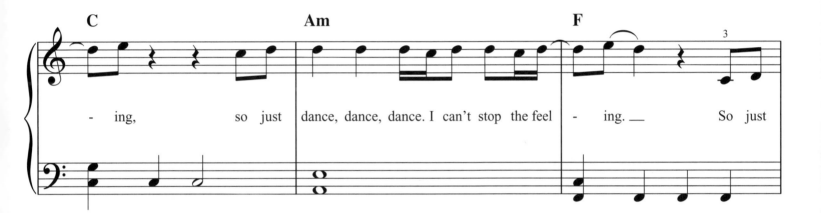

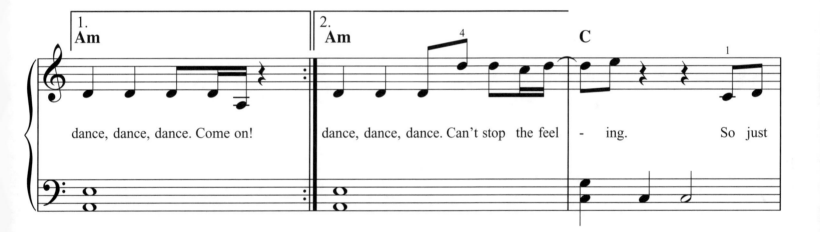

Oh. — Yeah, I can't stop the...

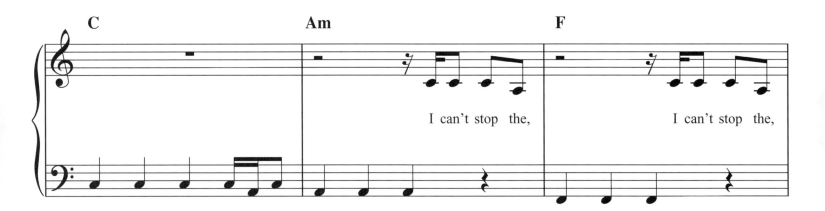

I can't stop the, I can't stop the,

I can't stop the, I can't stop the feel - ing.
Noth - ing I can see but you when you

dance, dance, dance. I feel a good, good creep - ing up on you, so just

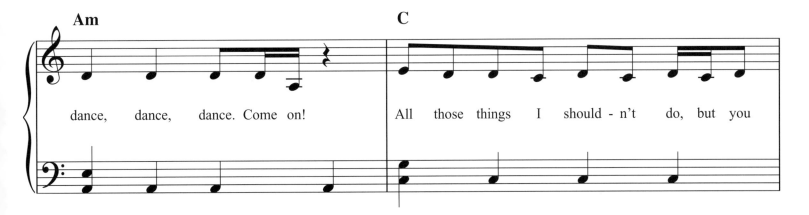

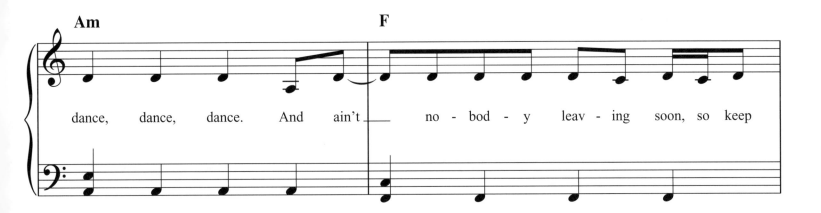

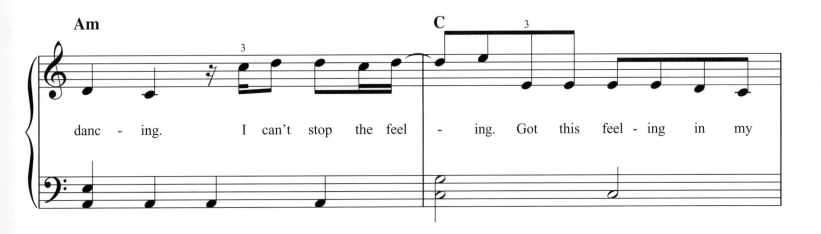

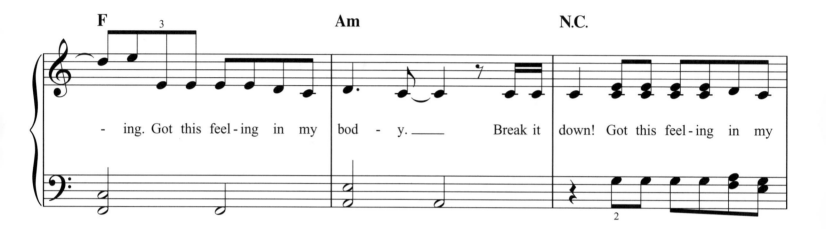

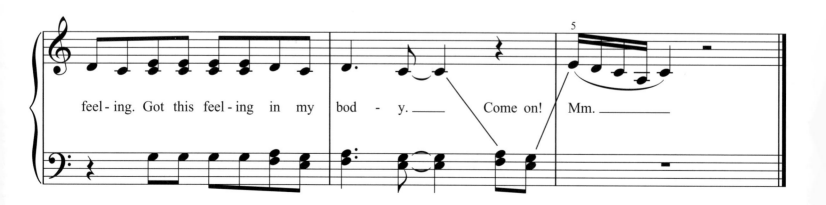

BUNDLE OF JOY

from INSIDE OUT

By MICHAEL GIACCHINO

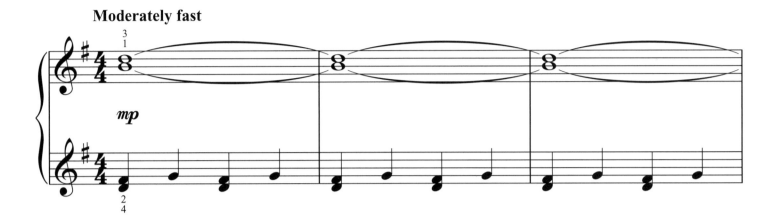

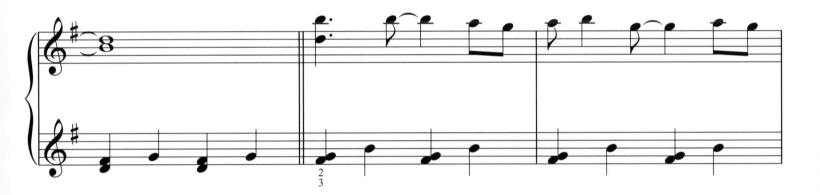

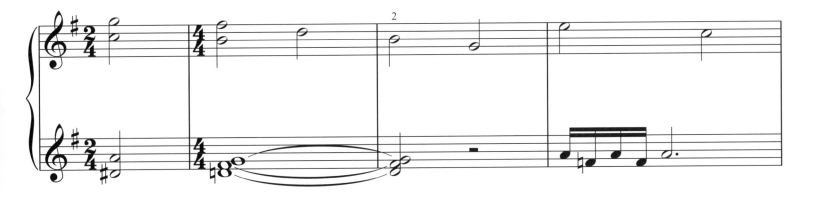

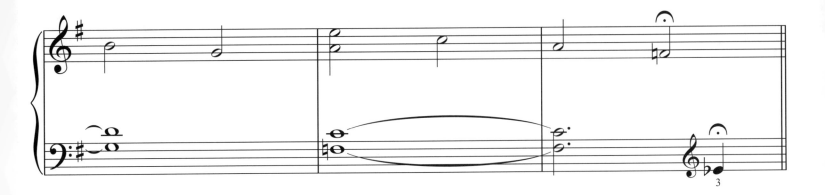

Moderately fast

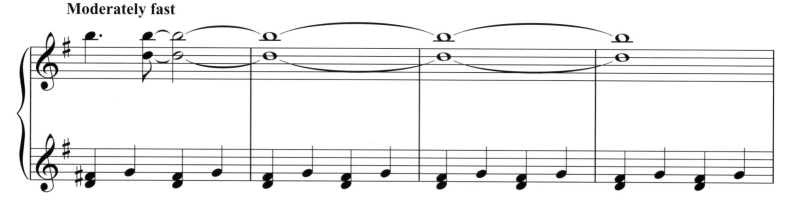

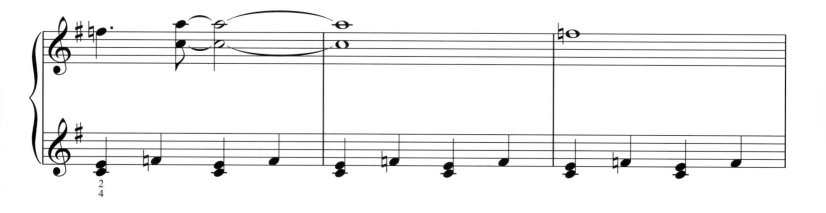

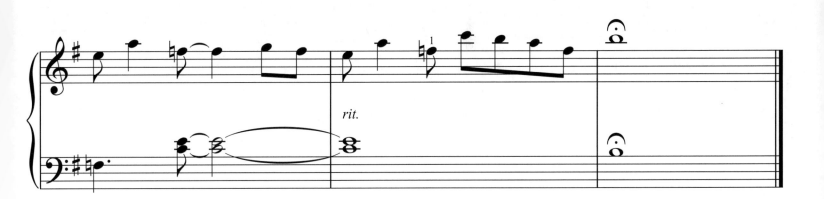

CITY OF STARS

from LA LA LAND

Music by JUSTIN HURWITZ
Lyrics by BENJ PASEK & JUSTIN PAUL

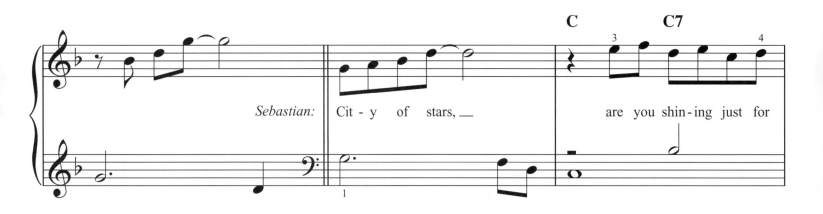

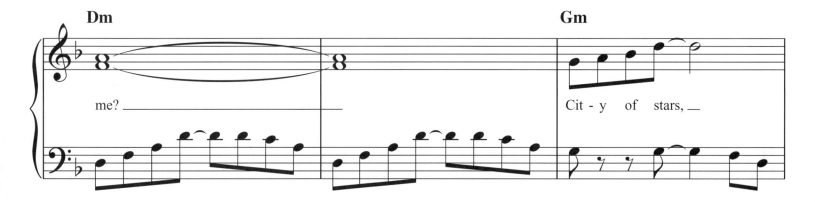

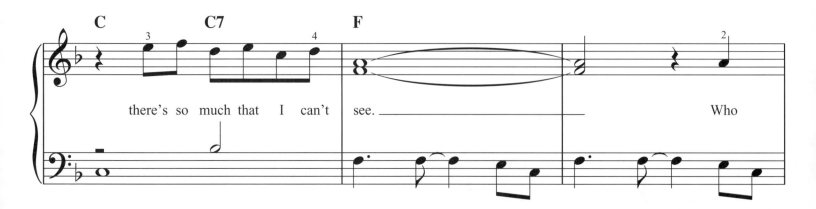

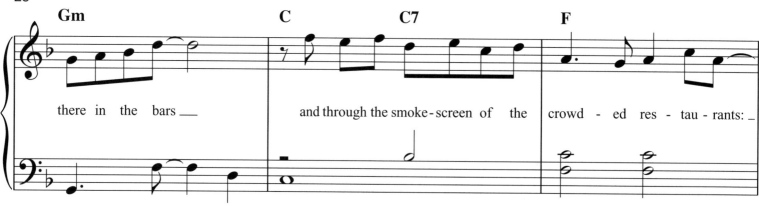

there in the bars ___ and through the smoke-screen of the crowd - ed res - tau - rants: _

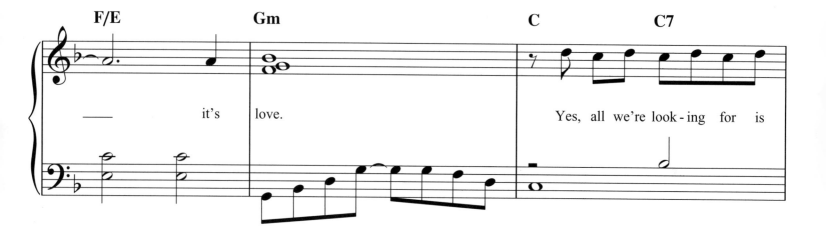

___ it's love. Yes, all we're look - ing for is

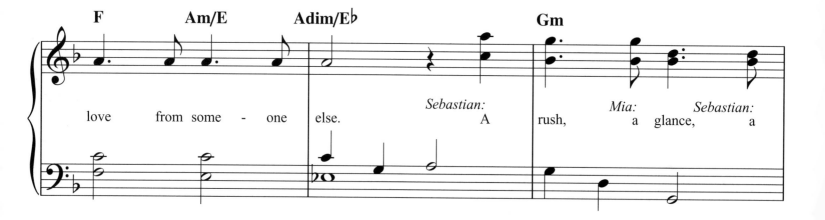

love from some - one else. *Sebastian:* A rush, *Mia:* a glance, *Sebastian:* a

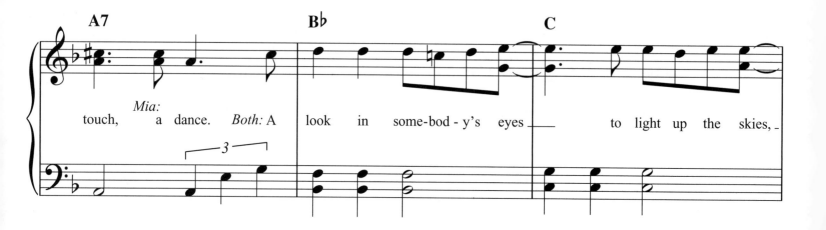

Mia:
touch, a dance. *Both:* A look in some-bod - y's eyes ___ to light up the skies, _

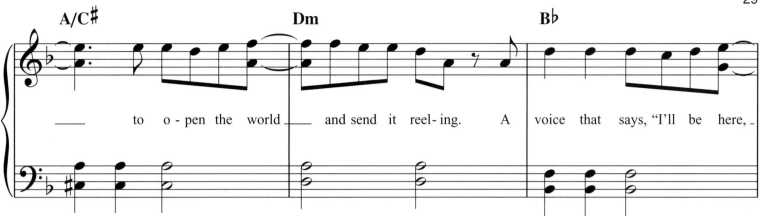

to o-pen the world___ and send it reel-ing. A voice that says, "I'll be here,_

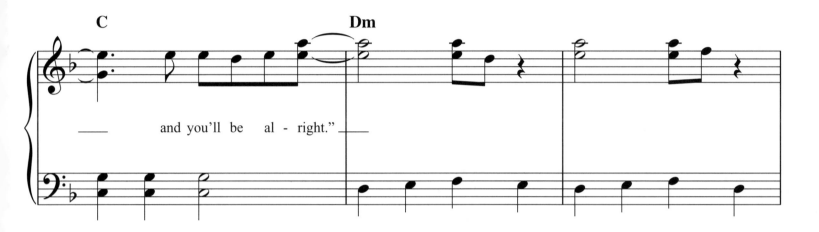

___ and you'll be al - right." ___

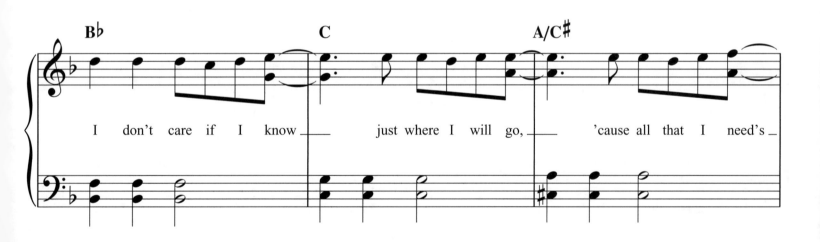

I don't care if I know___ just where I will go,___ 'cause all that I need's_

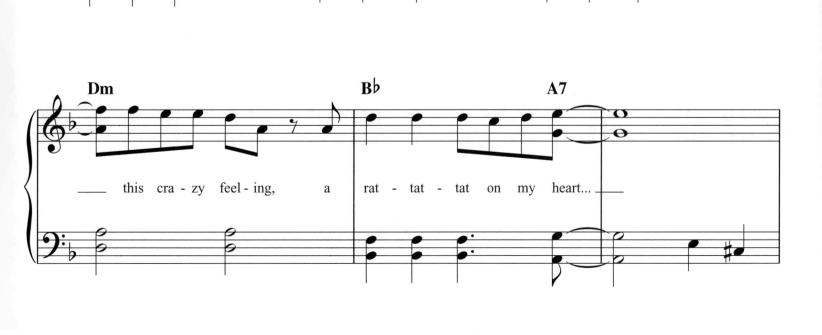

___ this cra-zy feel-ing, a rat - tat - tat on my heart...___

30

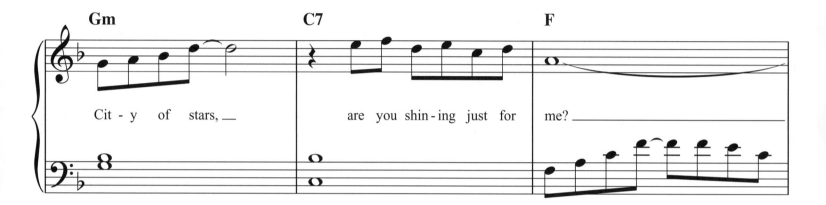

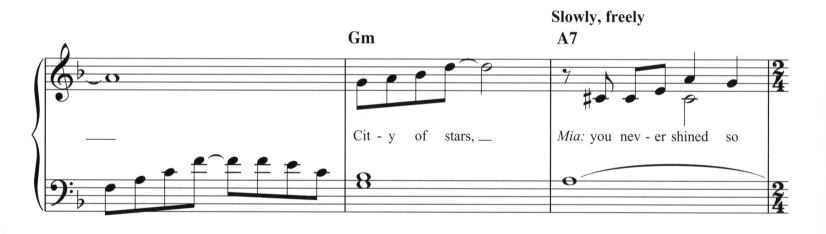

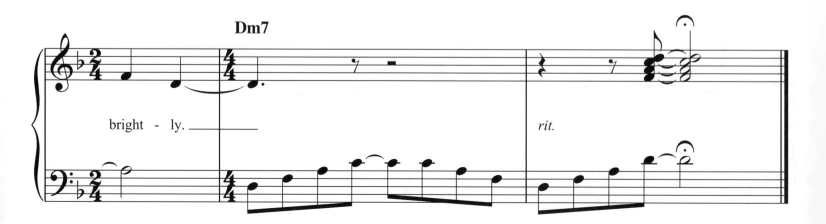

HOW FAR I'LL GO

from MOANA

Music and Lyrics by
LIN-MANUEL MIRANDA

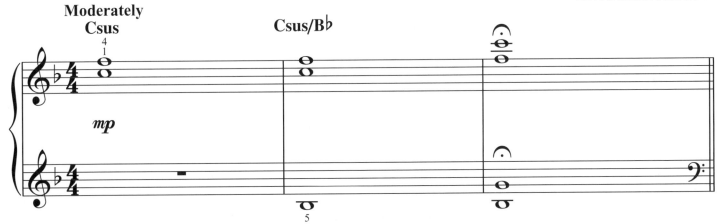

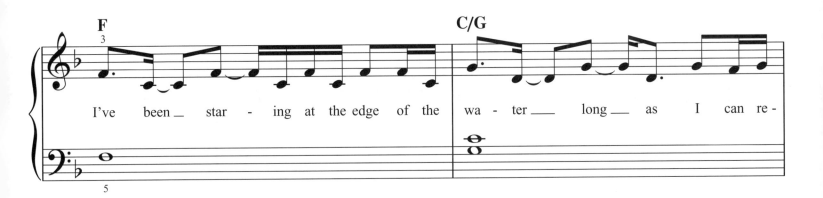

I've been __ star - ing at the edge of the wa - ter __ long __ as I can re -

mem - ber, __ nev - er real - ly know - ing why. I wish __ I could be the per - fect

daugh - ter, __ but I come back to the wa - ter __ no mat - ter how hard I try. Ev - 'ry

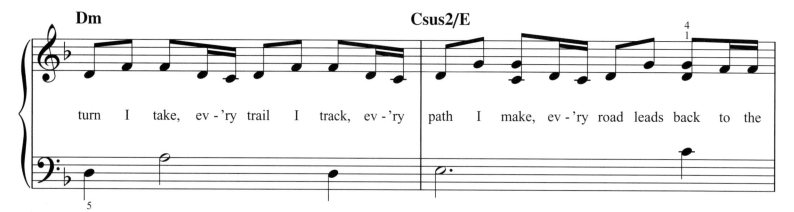

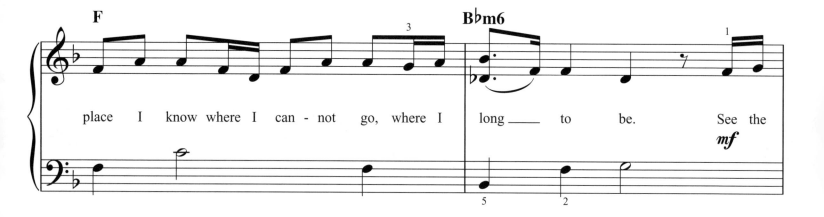

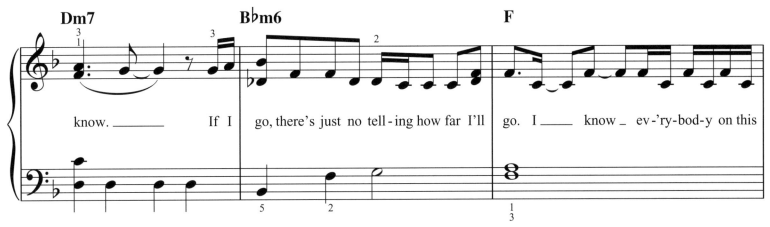

know. _____ If I | go, there's just no tell-ing how far I'll | go. I ____ know _ ev-'ry-bod-y on this

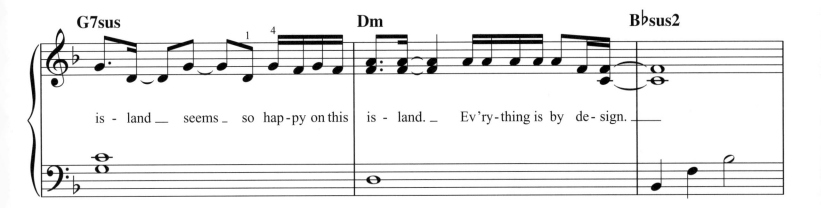

is - land __ seems _ so hap-py on this | is - land. _ Ev'-ry-thing is by de-sign. ___

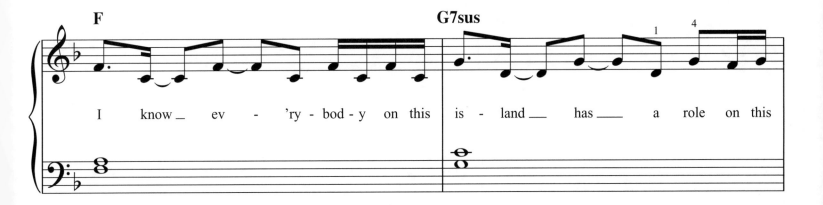

I know _ ev - 'ry - bod - y on this | is - land __ has ___ a role on this

is - land, __ so may-be I can roll with mine. ___ I can

34

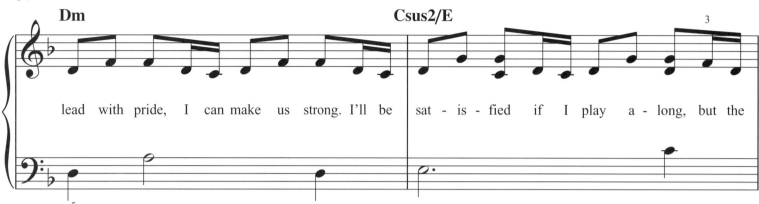

lead with pride, I can make us strong. I'll be | sat - is - fied if I play a - long, but the

voice in - side sings a dif - f'rent song. What is | wrong with me? | See the

light as it shines on the sea: it's blind | - ing, but no one | knows _____ how deep it

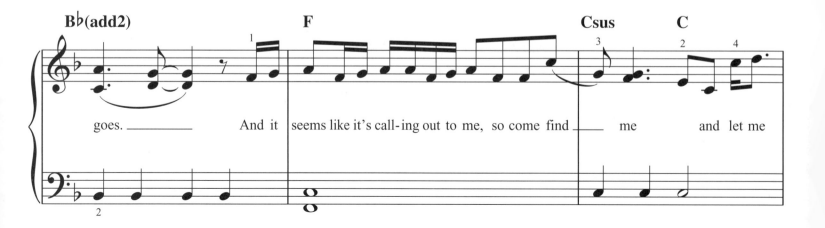

goes. _____ And it | seems like it's call-ing out to me, so come find ___ me and let me

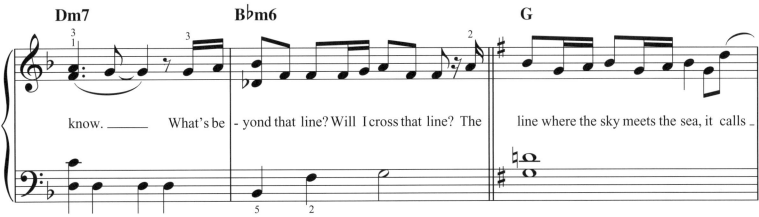

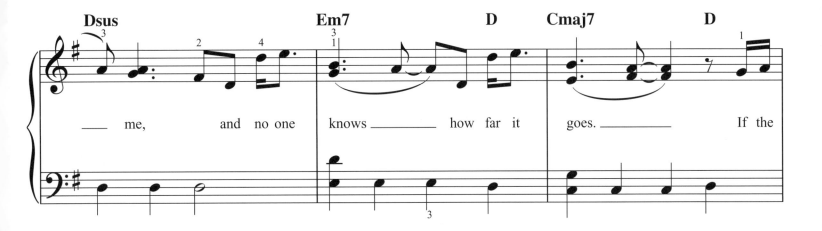

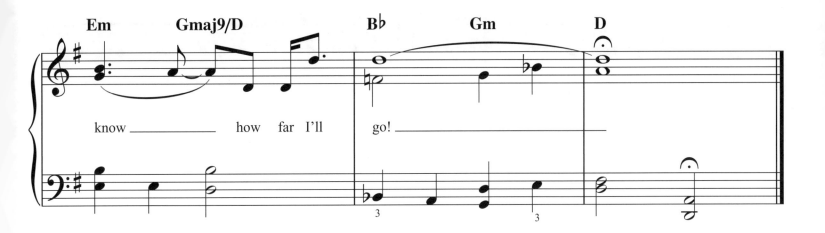

EVERMORE
from BEAUTY AND THE BEAST

Music by ALAN MENKEN
Lyrics by TIM RICE

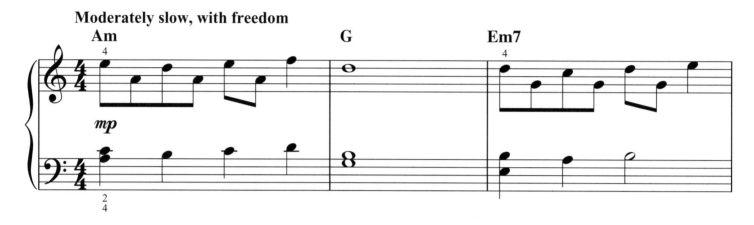

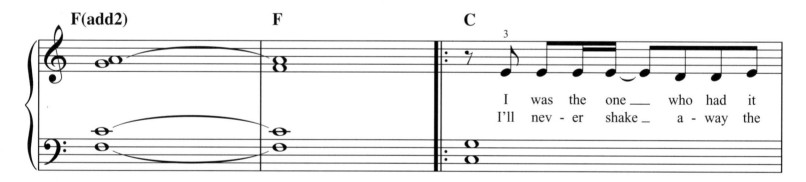

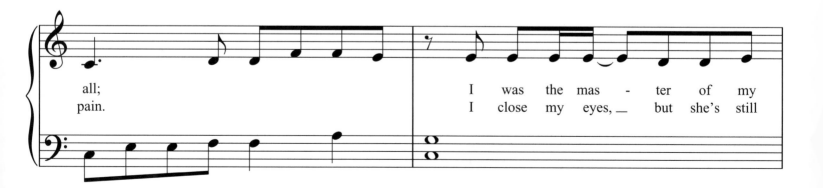

fate.
there.

I nev-er need-ed an-y-bod-y in my life;
I let her steal in-to my mel-an-chol-y heart;

I learned the truth ___ too late.
it's more than I ___ can

1.
bear. ___

2.

___ Now I know she'll nev-er leave me, e-ven

as she runs a-way. She will still tor-ment ___ me,

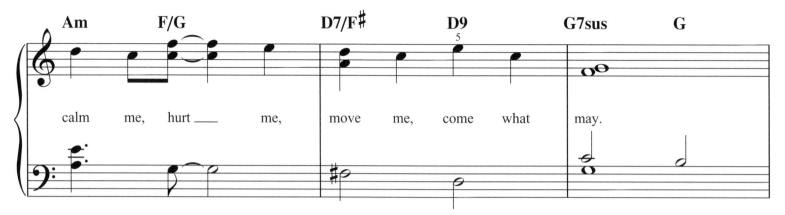

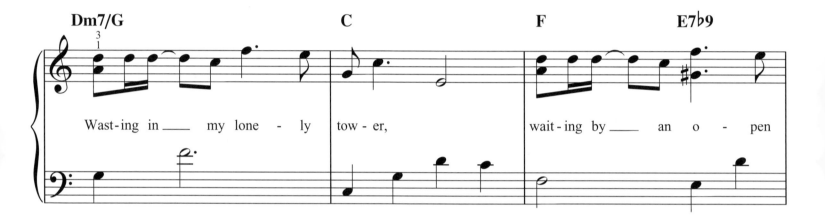

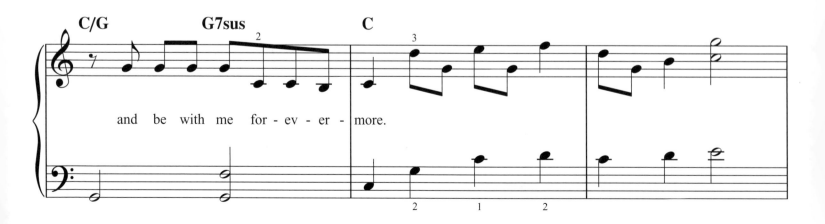

I rage a - gainst _ the trials of love. I curse the fad - ing of the

light. Though she's al - read - y flown so far be - yond my reach,

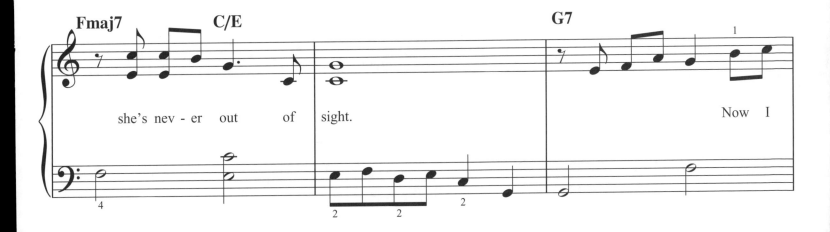

she's nev - er out of sight. Now I

know she'll nev - er leave me, e - ven as she fades from

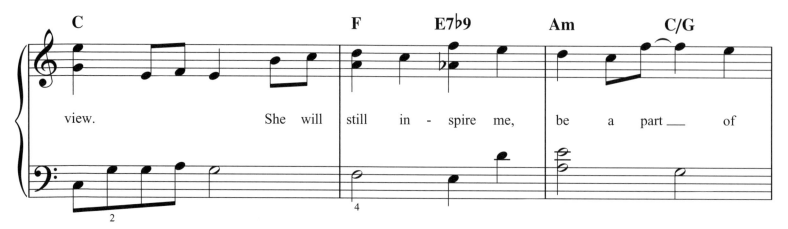

C   F   E7♭9   Am   C/G

view.   She will still in - spire me,   be a part ___ of

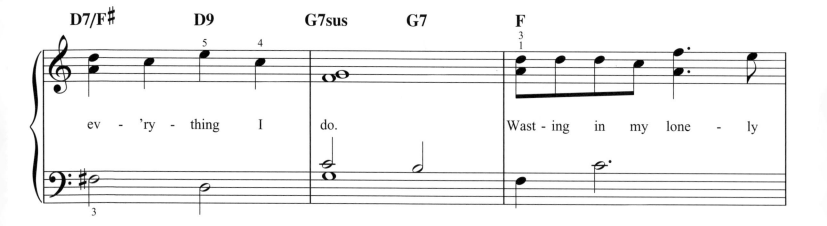

D7/F♯   D9   G7sus   G7   F

ev - 'ry - thing I   do.   Wast - ing in my lone - ly

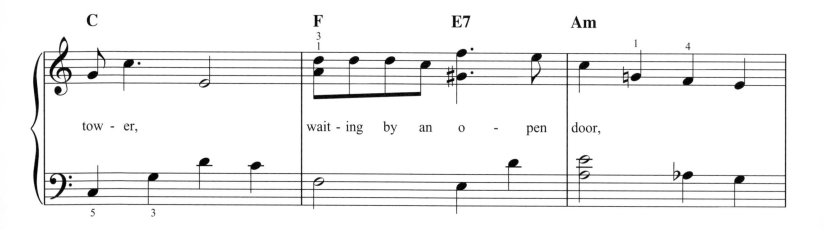

C   F   E7   Am

tow - er,   wait - ing by an o - pen door,

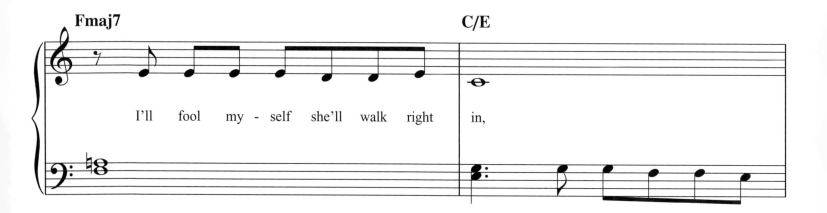

Fmaj7   C/E

I'll fool my - self she'll walk right   in,

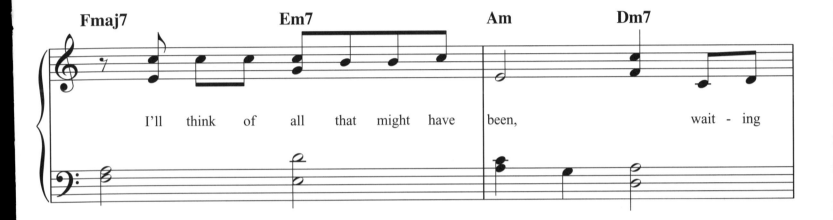

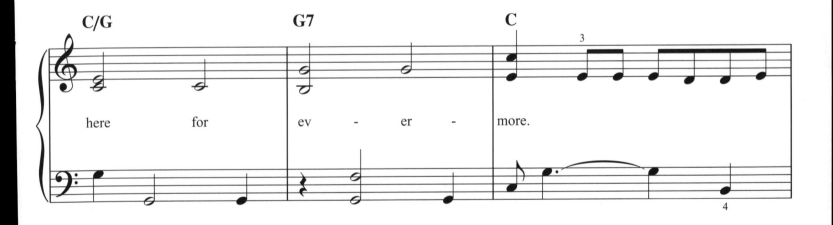

EVERYTHING IS AWESOME

(Awesome Remix!!!)
from THE LEGO MOVIE

Words by SHAWN PATTERSON
Music by ANDREW SAMBERG,
JORMA TACCONE, AKIVA SCHAFFER,
JOSHUA BARTHOLOMEW, LISA HARRITON
and SHAWN PATTERSON

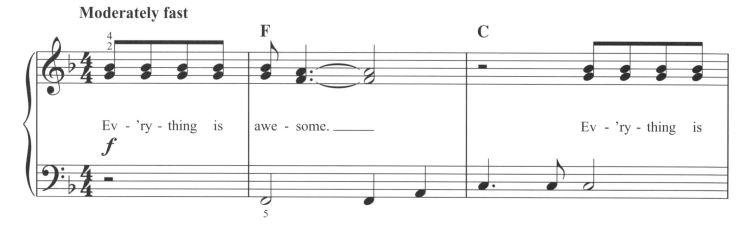

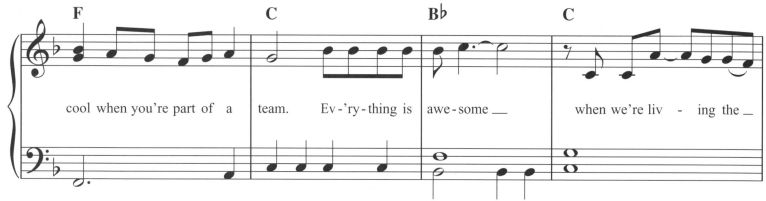

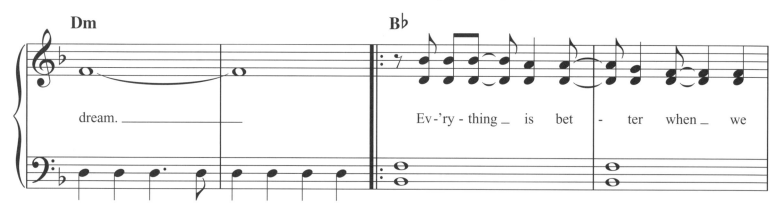

gon - na win ___ for - ev - er. Let's par - ty for - ev - er. ___

We're the same, ___ I'm like you, ___ you're like me. ___ We're all work - ing in har - mon - y. ___

___ Ev - 'ry - thing is awe - some. ___ Ev - 'ry - thing is

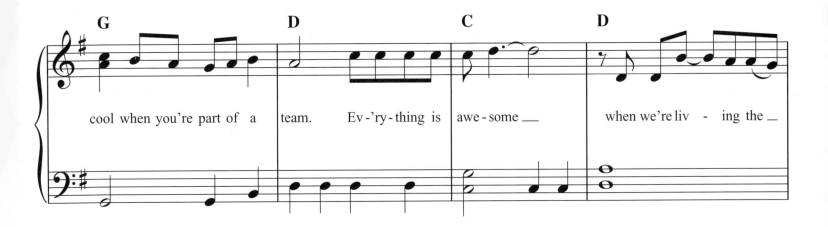

cool when you're part of a team. Ev - 'ry - thing is awe - some ___ when we're liv - ing the ___

44

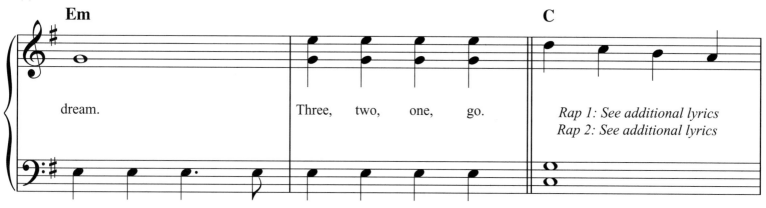

dream.

Three, two, one, go.

Rap 1: See additional lyrics
Rap 2: See additional lyrics

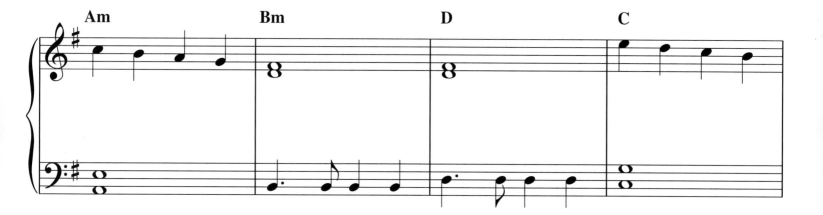

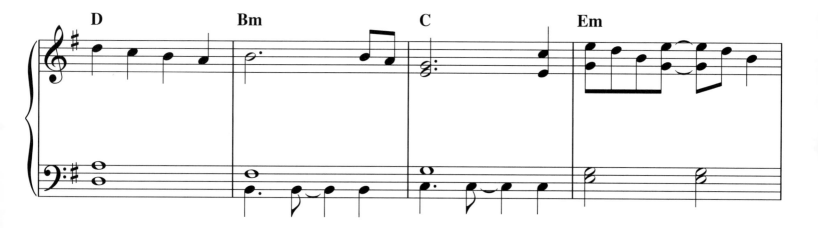

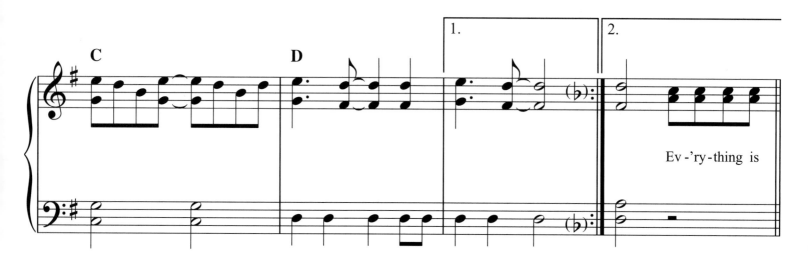

Ev -'ry-thing is

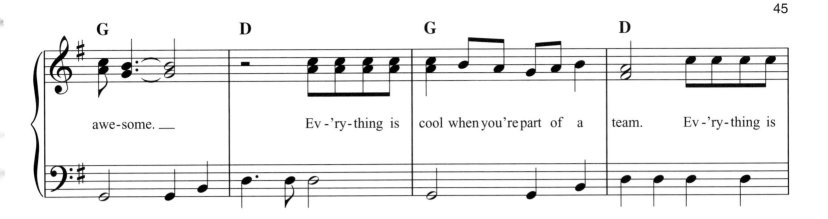

awe-some. ___   Ev-'ry-thing is cool when you're part of a team. Ev-'ry-thing is

awe-some ___   when we're liv - ing the ___ dream.

Rap 1:

Have you heard the news? Everyone's talkin'.
Life is good 'cause everything's awesome.
Lost my job, there's a new opportunity,
I feel more awesome than an awesome possum,
Dip my body in chocolate frostin'
Three years later wash off the frostin'
Smellin' like a blossom, everything is awesome.
Stepped in mud, got new brown shoes.
It's awesome to win and it's awesome to lose.

Rap 2:

Blue skies, bouncy springs,
We just named two awesome things.
A Nobel prize, a piece of string,
You know what's awesome? EVERYTHING!
Dogs with fleas,
Allergies,
A book of Greek antiquities,
Brand new pants, a very old vest,
Awesome items are the best.
Trees, frogs, clogs, they're awesome!
Rocks, clocks and socks, they're awesome!
Figs, jigs, and twigs, that's awesome!
Everything you see or think or say is awesome!

LAVA
from LAVA

Music and Lyrics by
JAMES FORD MURPHY

Easy half-time feel

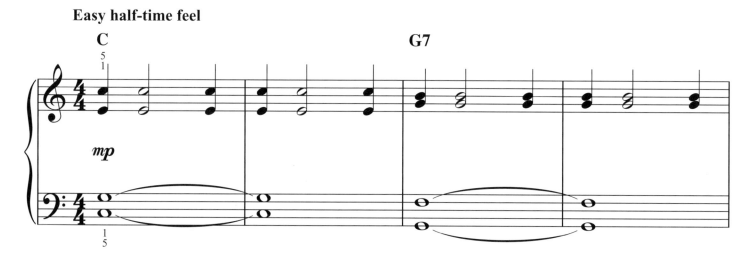

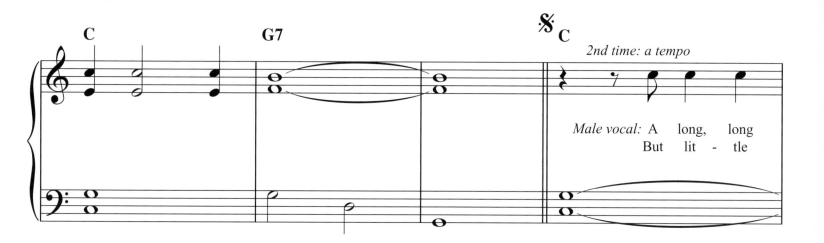

2nd time: a tempo

Male vocal: A long, long
But lit - tle

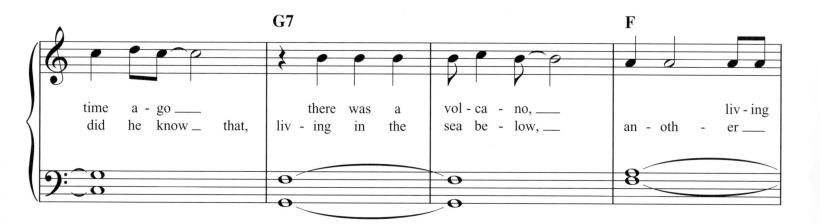

time a - go ___ there was a vol - ca - no, ___ liv - ing
did he know ___ that, liv - ing in the sea be - low, ___ an - oth - er

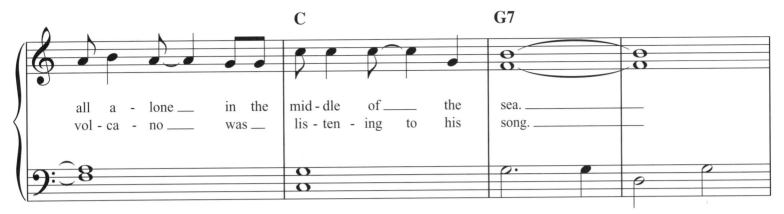

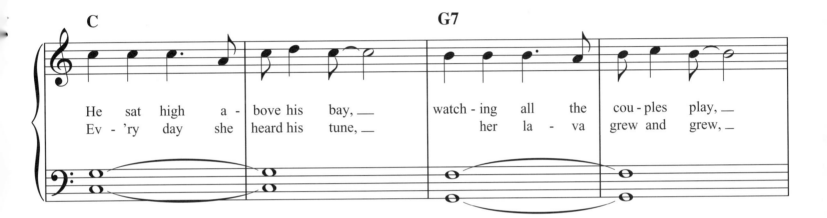

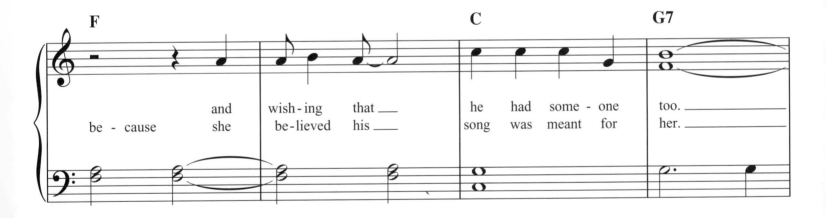

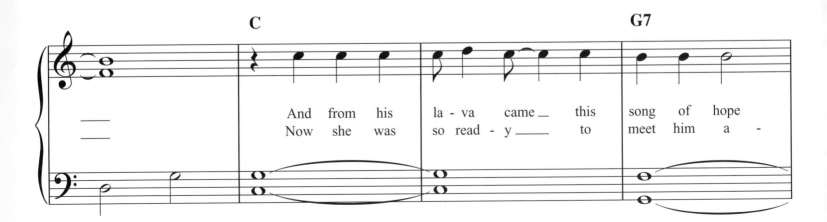

48

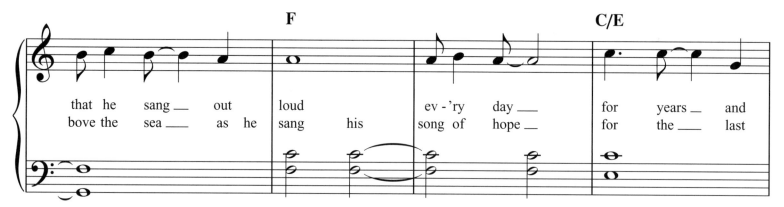

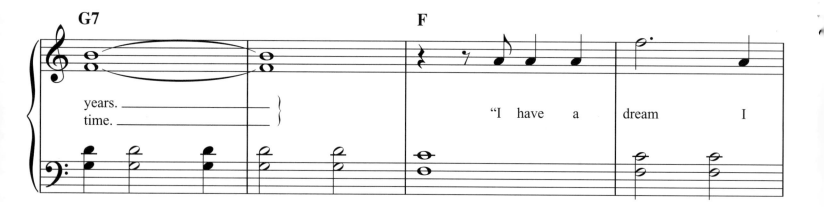

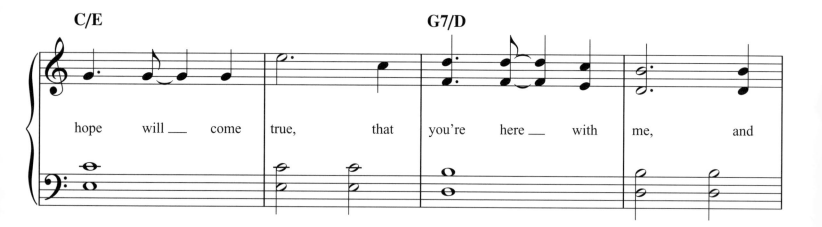

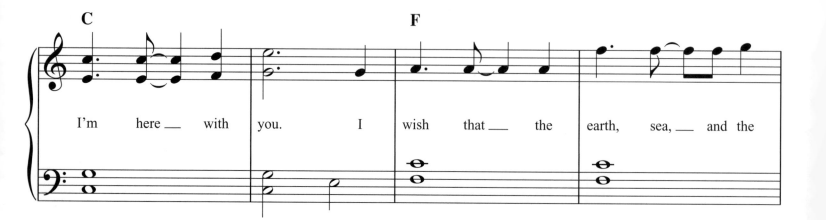

To Coda

sky up __ a - bove - a __ will send me some - one to

Slower

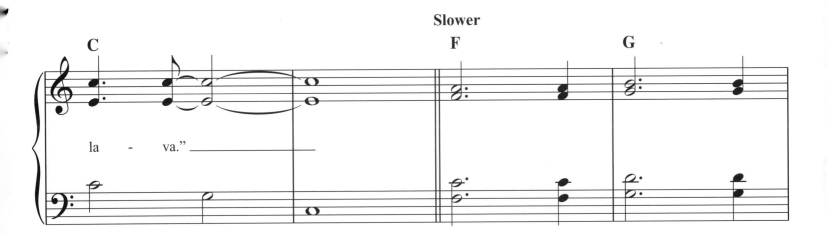

la - va." _____

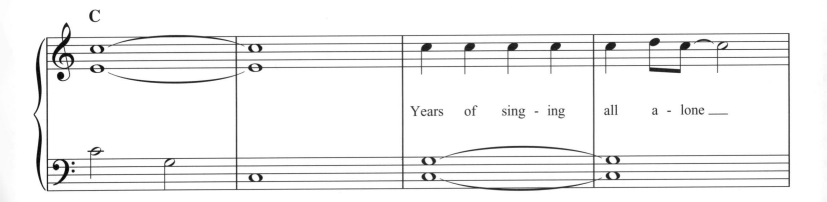

Years of sing - ing all a - lone __

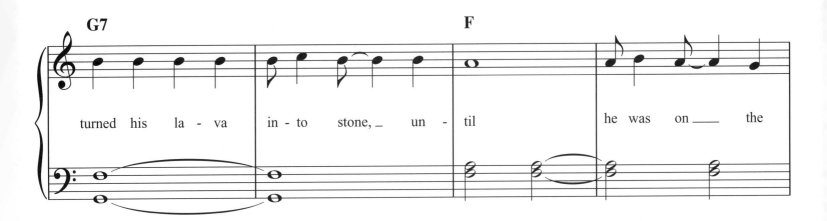

turned his la - va in - to stone, __ un - til he was on __ the

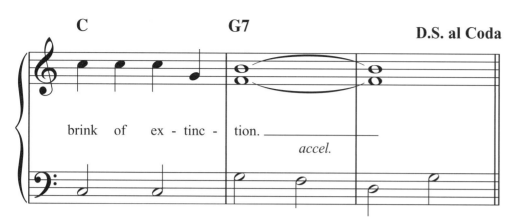

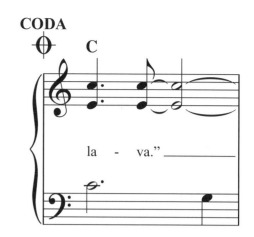

brink of ex - tinc - tion. _____

accel.

la - va." _____

_____ Ris - ing from the

sea be - low ___ stood a love - ly vol - ca - no, ___ look - ing

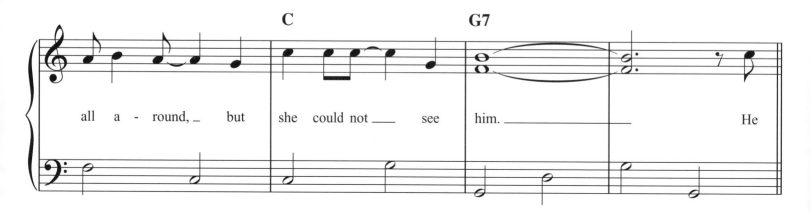

all a - round, _ but she could not ___ see him. _____ He

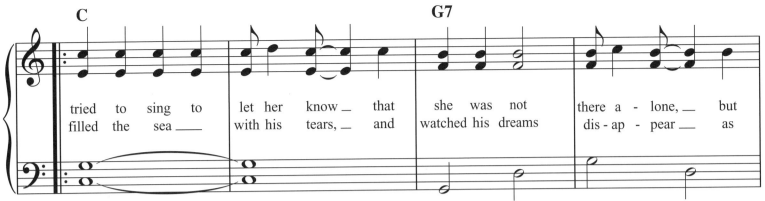

tried to sing to ... let her know __ that ... she was not ... there a - lone, __ but
filled the sea __ ... with his tears, __ and ... watched his dreams ... dis - ap - pear __ as

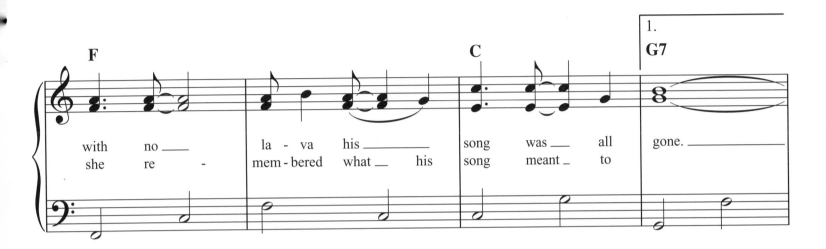

with no __ ... la - va his __ ... song was __ all ... gone. __
she re - ... mem - bered what __ his ... song meant __ to

__ He ... her. __ ... *Female vocal:* "I have a

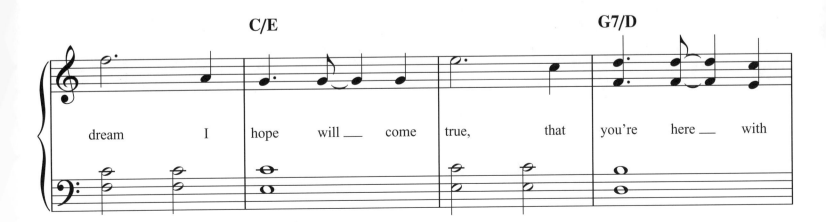

dream I ... hope will __ come ... true, ... that ... you're here __ with

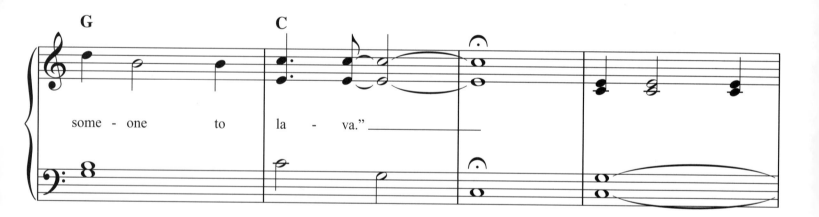

bove the sea. ___
their new home, ___

F All ___ to-geth-er now ___ their
and when you vis-it them ___

C la - va grew and
this is what they

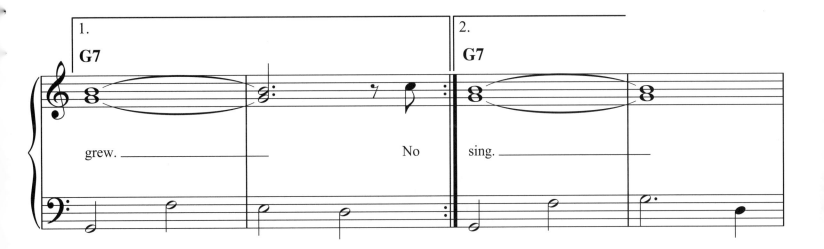

1.
G7 grew. _____ No

2.
G7 sing. _____

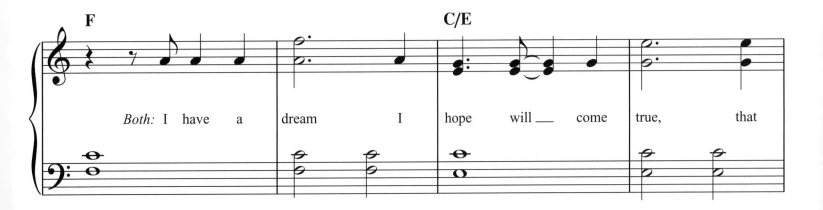

F *Both:* I have a dream I

C/E hope will ___ come true, that

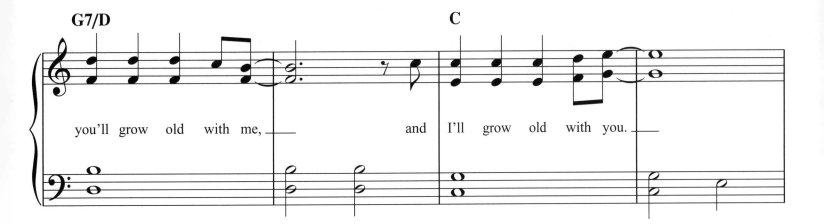

G7/D you'll grow old with me, ___

C and I'll grow old with you. ___

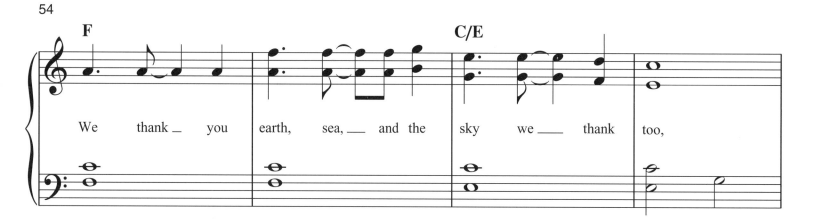

We thank ___ you earth, sea, ___ and the sky we ___ thank too,

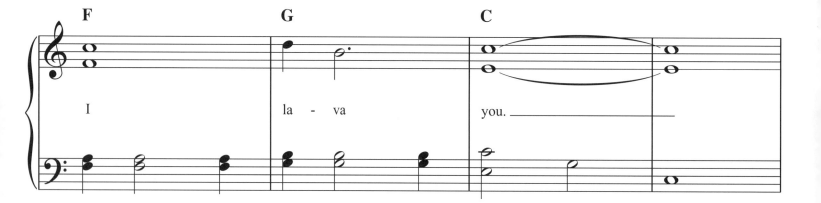

I la - va you. _____

I la - va you. _____

A little slower

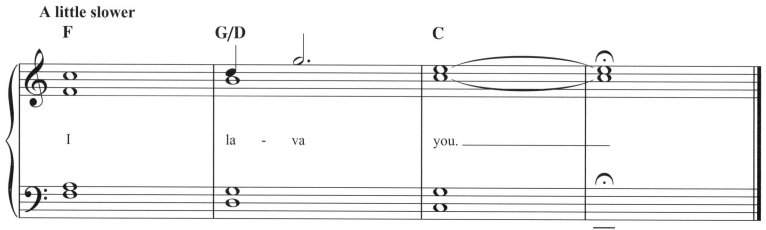

I la - va you. _____

IN SUMMER
from FROZEN

Music and Lyrics by KRISTEN ANDERSON-LOPEZ
and ROBERT LOPEZ

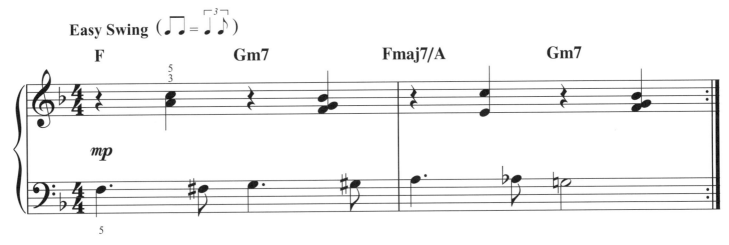

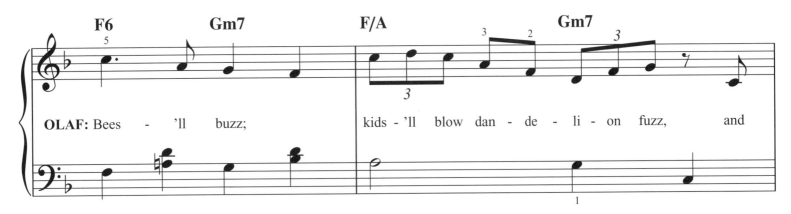

OLAF: Bees - 'll buzz; kids - 'll blow dan - de - li - on fuzz, and

I'll be do - ing what - ev - er snow does in sum - mer.

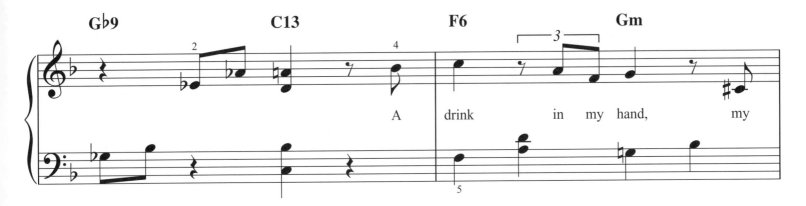

A drink in my hand, my

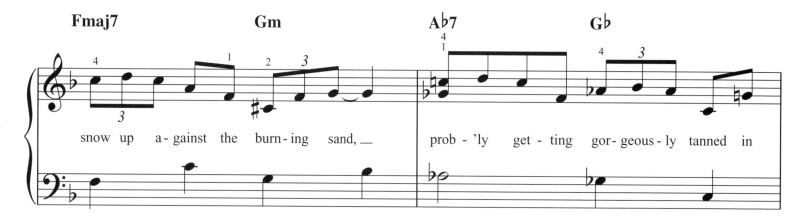

snow up a-gainst the burn-ing sand, __ prob - 'ly get - ting gor- geous - ly tanned in

sum - mer. __ I'll fi - n'lly see a sum - mer breeze __ blow a-

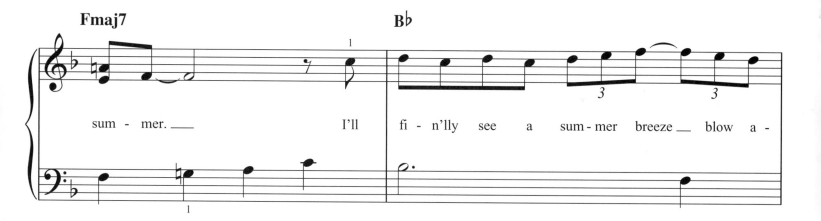

way a win - ter storm, __ and find out what hap - pens to sol - id wat - er when

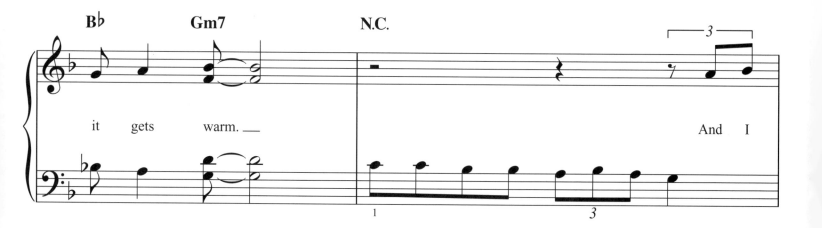

it gets warm. __ And I

can't wait to see what my bud - dies all think of me. Just im -

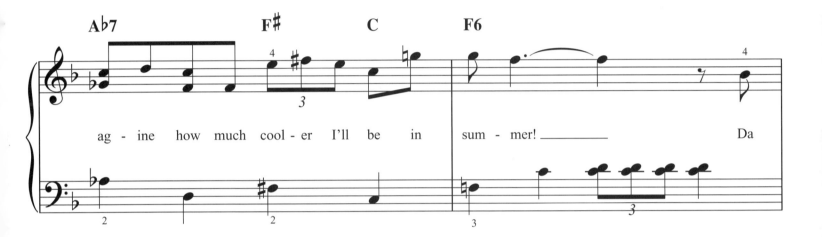

ag - ine how much cool - er I'll be in sum - mer! _____ Da

da, da doo, a ba ba ba ba ba boo. __ The

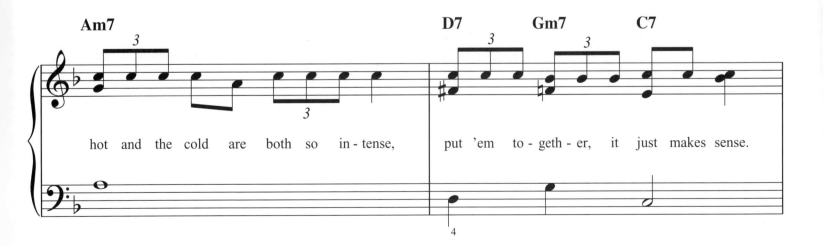

hot and the cold are both so in - tense, put 'em to - geth - er, it just makes sense.

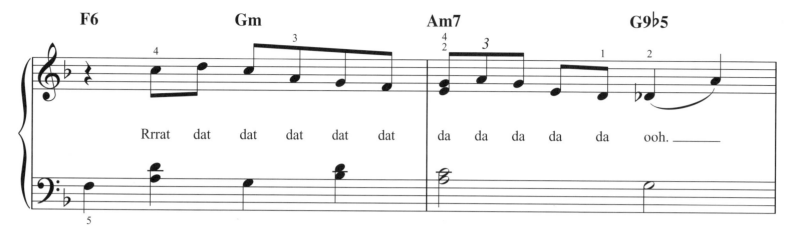

F6   **Gm**   **Am7**   **G9♭5**

Rrrat dat dat dat dat dat da da da da da ooh. _____

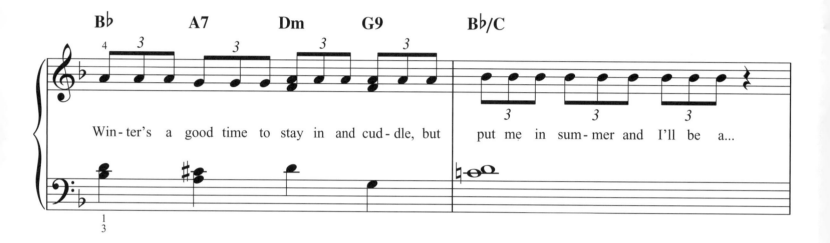

B♭   **A7**   **Dm**   **G9**   **B♭/C**

Win-ter's a good time to stay in and cud-dle, but put me in sum-mer and I'll be a...

N.C.   **B♭6**

(Spoken:) happy snowman!   *(Sung:)* When life gets rough, I like to

F   **Dm**   **G**

hold on _____ to my dream of re - lax - ing in the sum-mer sun, ___ just

let - tin' off steam. ___   Oh, the sky   will be blue,   and

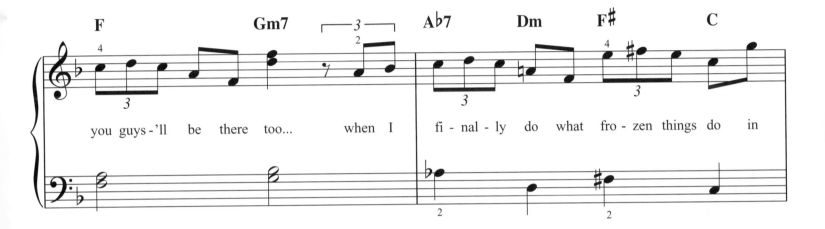

you guys-'ll be there too...   when I   fi - nal - ly do what fro - zen things do in

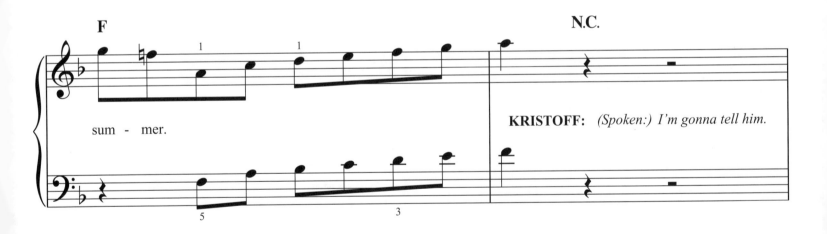

sum - mer.   **KRISTOFF:** *(Spoken:) I'm gonna tell him.*

ANNA: *Don't you dare!*   **OLAF:** In   sum - mer! ___

LINUS AND LUCY
from THE PEANUTS MOVIE

By VINCE GUARALDI

SOMETHING WILD

from PETE'S DRAGON

Words and Music by LINDSEY STIRLING,
ANDREW McMAHON, PETER HANNA
and TAYLOR BIRD

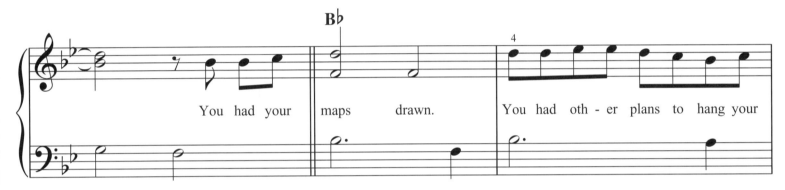

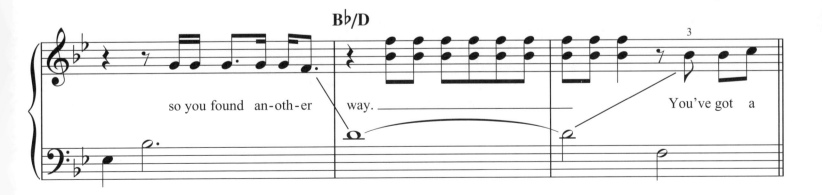

big   heart.   The   way you see the world, _ it got you   this   far.
past   can   make the ground be - neath _ you feel like quick -   sand.

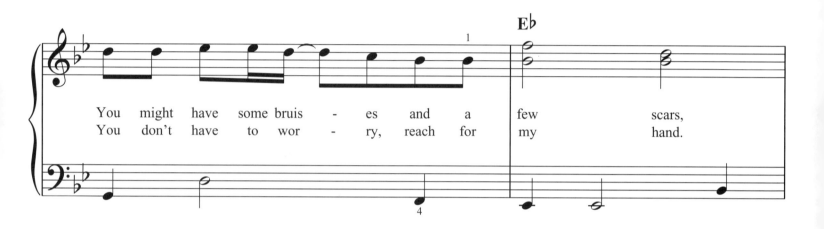

You might have some bruis -   es   and   a   few   scars,
You   don't have to wor -   ry, reach for   my   hand.

but you know you're gon - na be o -   kay.
Yeah, I know you're gon - na be o -   kay.

And e - ven though _ you're scared, you're strong-er than _ you know.   If you're

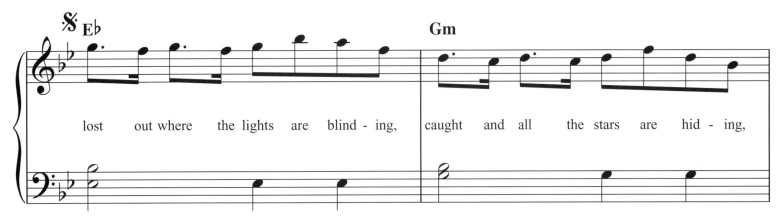

lost out where the lights are blind - ing, caught and all the stars are hid - ing,

that's when some-thing wild _ calls you home, home. _ If you face the fear that keeps you fro - zen,

chase the sky in - to the o - cean, that's when some-thing wild _ calls you home, home. _ Whoa, _

oh, _____ oh, _____ oh, _____

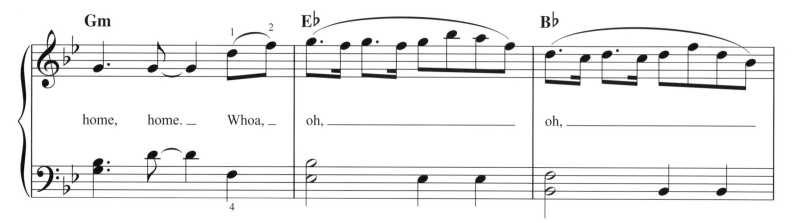

Calls you home. Calls you

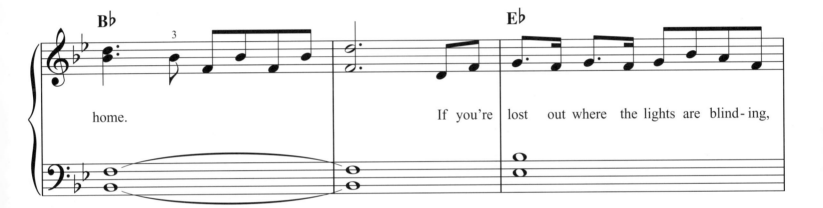

home. If you're lost out where the lights are blind-ing,

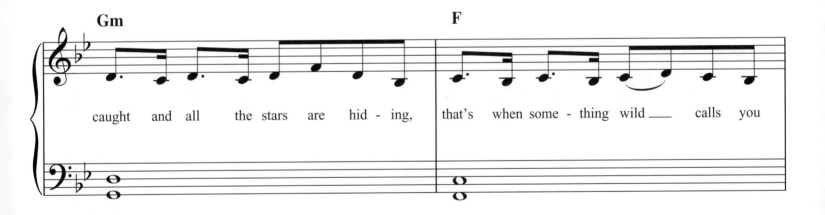

caught and all the stars are hid-ing, that's when some-thing wild ___ calls you

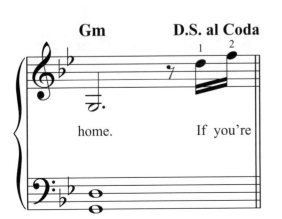

home. If you're

home, home. _

REY'S THEME
from STAR WARS: THE FORCE AWAKENS

Music by JOHN WILLIAMS

Moderately, steadily

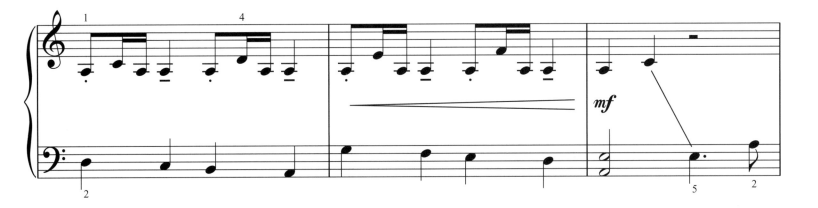

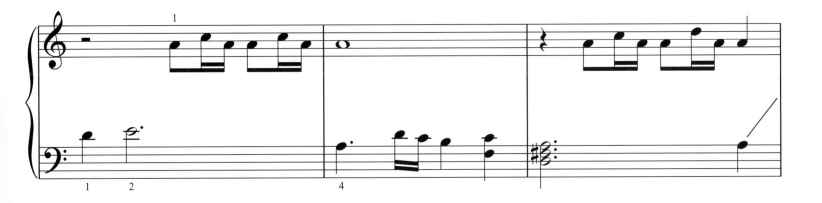

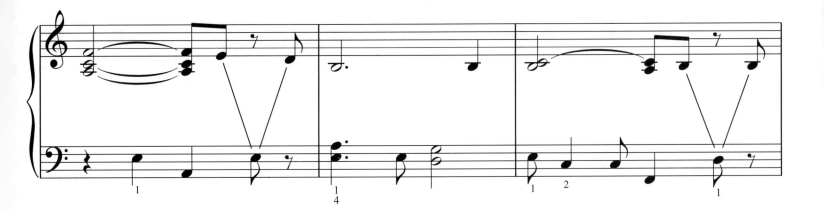

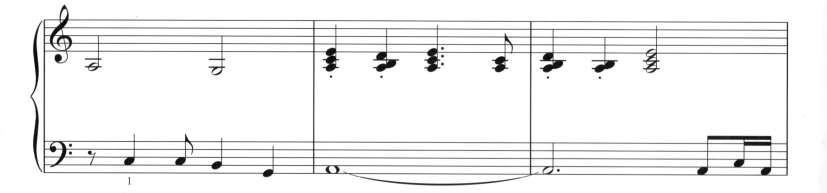

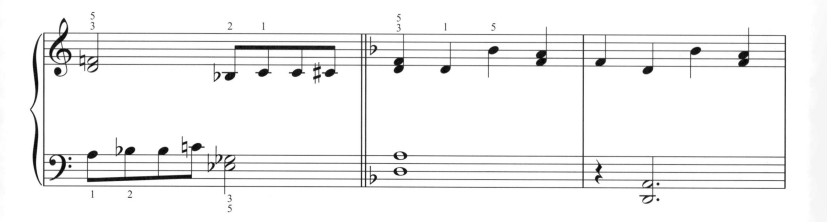

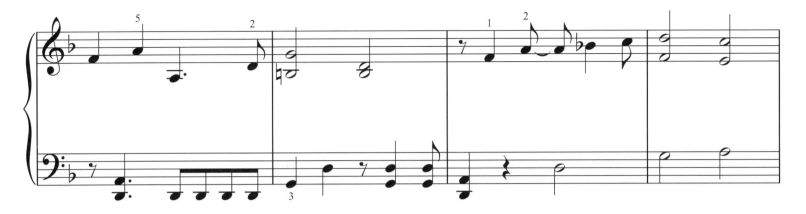

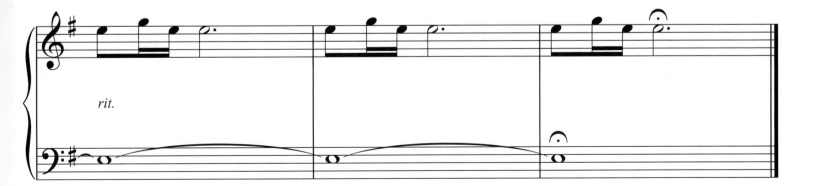

SPIRIT IN THE SKY

featured in GUARDIANS OF THE GALAXY

Words and Music by
NORMAN GREENBAUM

Moderate Rock Shuffle

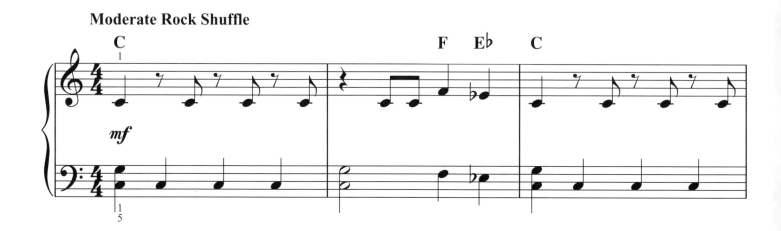

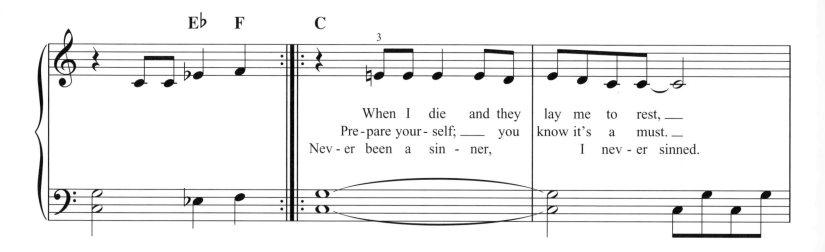

When I die and they lay me to rest, ___
Pre-pare your-self; ___ you know it's a must. ___
Nev-er been a sin-ner, I nev-er sinned.

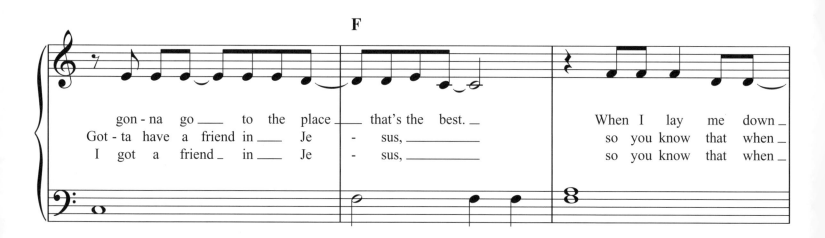

gon-na go ___ to the place ___ that's the best. ___   When I lay me down ___
Got-ta have a friend in ___ Je - sus, ___   so you know that when ___
I got a friend ___ in ___ Je - sus, ___   so you know that when ___

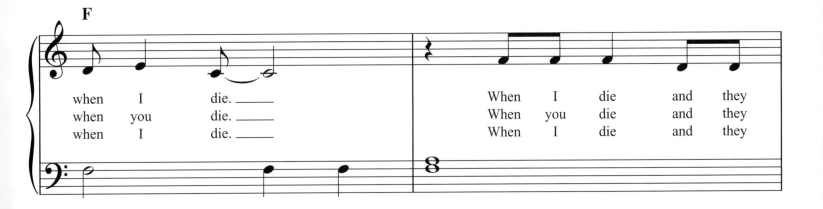

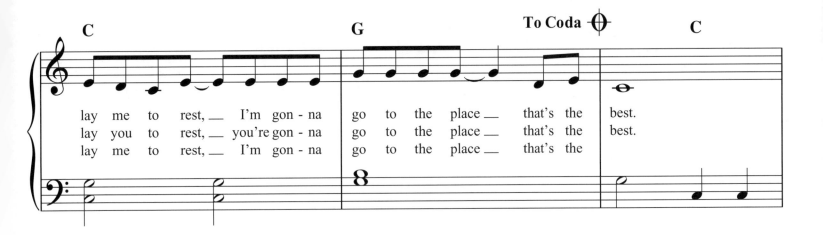

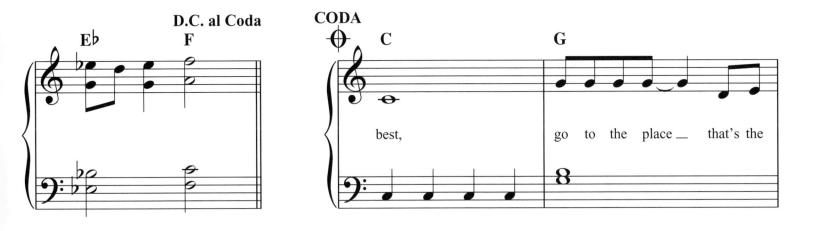

STRONG
from CINDERELLA

Words and Music by PATRICK DOYLE,
KENNETH BRANAGH and TOMMY DANVERS

Moderately, in 2

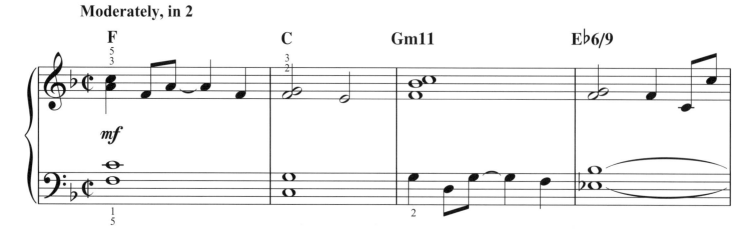

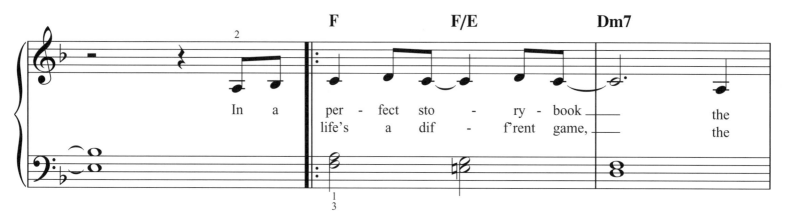

In a per - fect sto - ry - book ___ the
life's a dif - f'rent game, ___ the

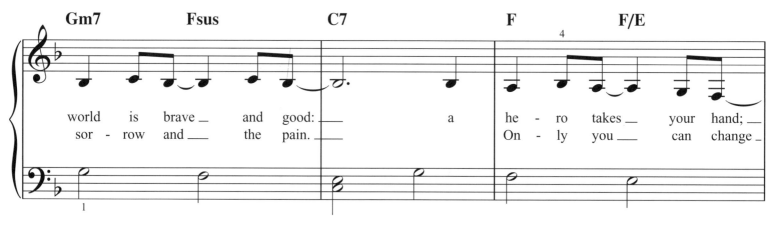

world is brave ___ and good: ___ a
sor - row and ___ the pain. ___

he - ro takes ___ your hand; ___
On - ly you ___ can change ___

sweet ___ love will fol - low. But ___
your world to - mor -

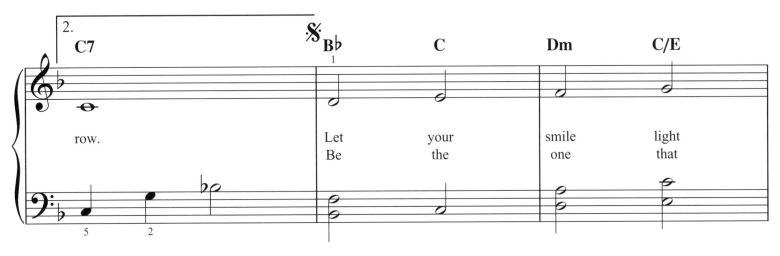

row.

Let your smile light
Be the one that

up the _____ sky;
res - cues _____ you.

keep your
Through the

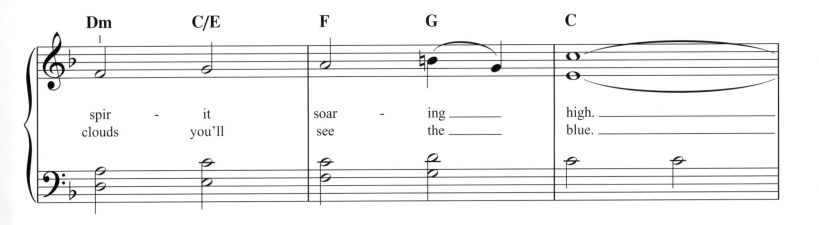

spir - it
clouds you'll

soar - ing _____
see the _____

high. _____
blue. _____

Trust in _____ your heart, and _____ your

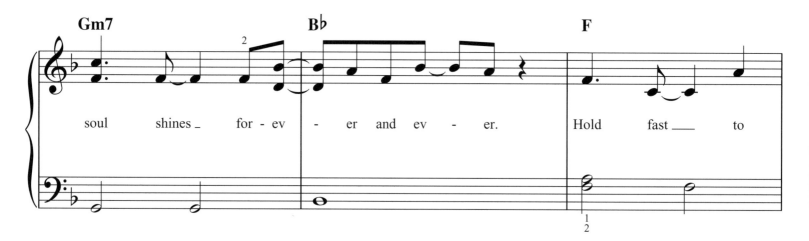

soul   shines __ for - ev - er   and ev - er.   Hold   fast ___ to

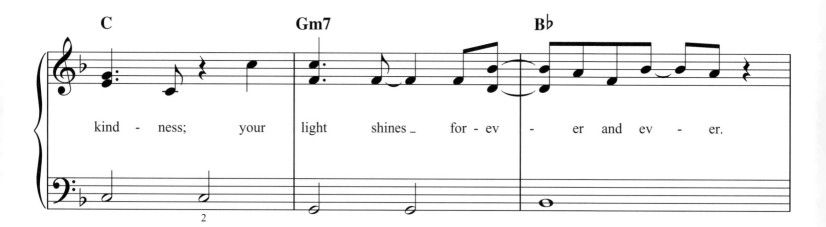

kind - ness;   your   light   shines __ for - ev - er   and ev - er.

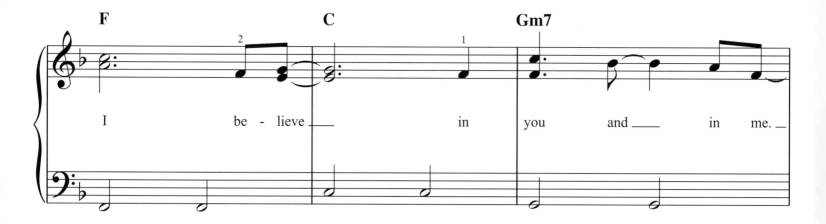

I   be - lieve ___   in   you   and ___ in   me. __

___   We   are

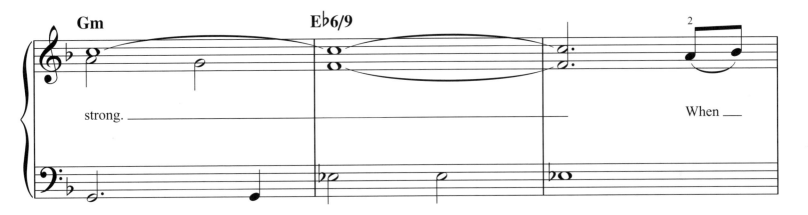

strong. _____ When ___

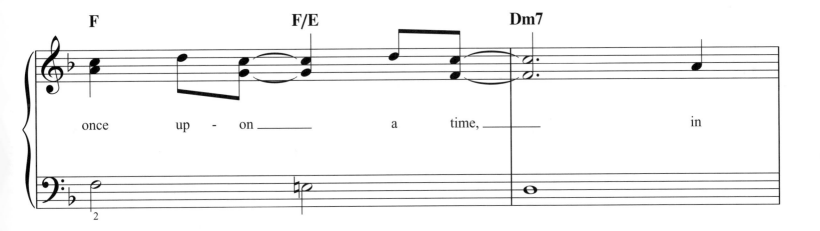

once up - on ___ ___ a time, ___ in

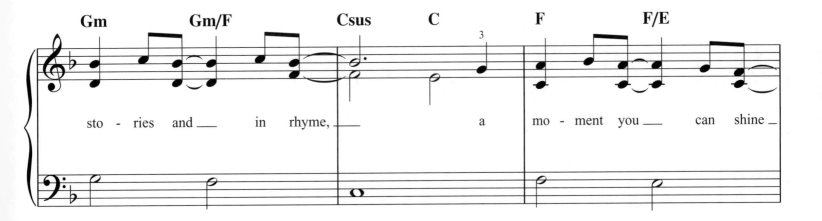

sto - ries and ___ in rhyme, ___ a mo - ment you ___ can shine ___

D.S. al Coda

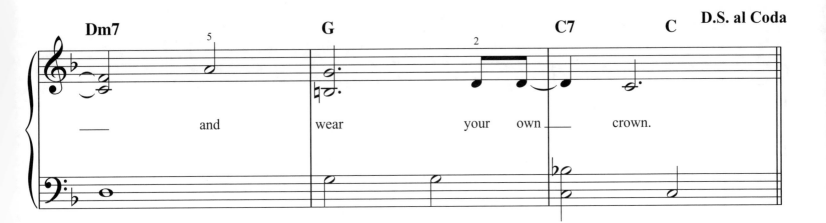

___ and wear your own ___ crown.

CODA

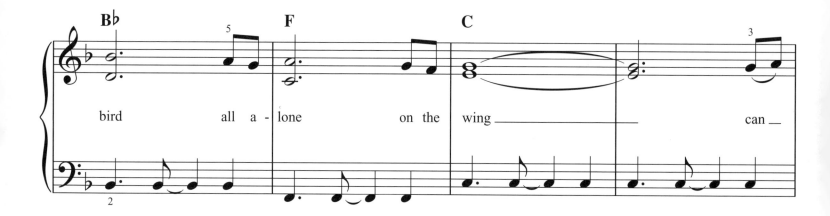

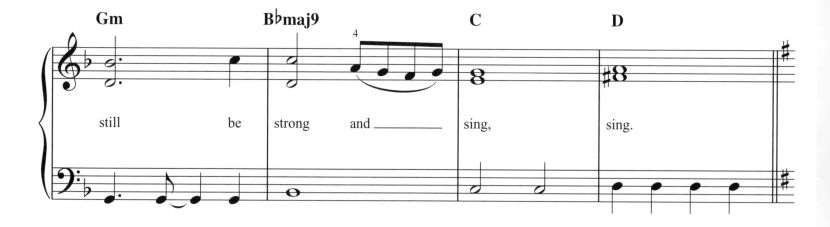

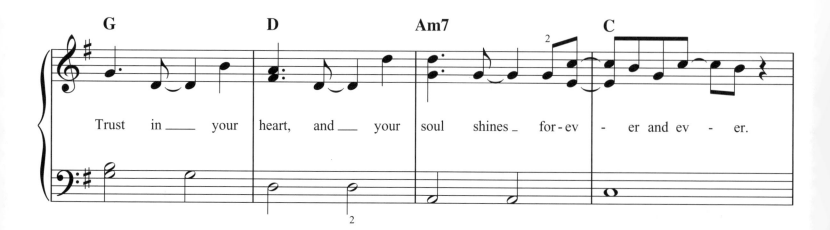

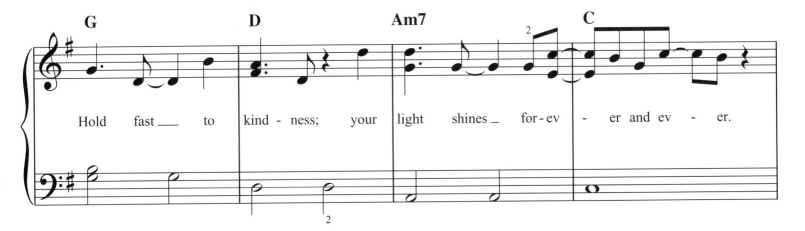

Hold fast ___ to kind - ness; your light shines ___ for - ev - - er and ev - - er.

I be - lieve ___ in you and ___ in me. ___

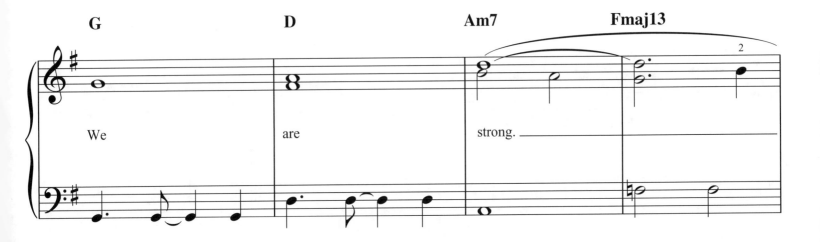

We are strong. ___

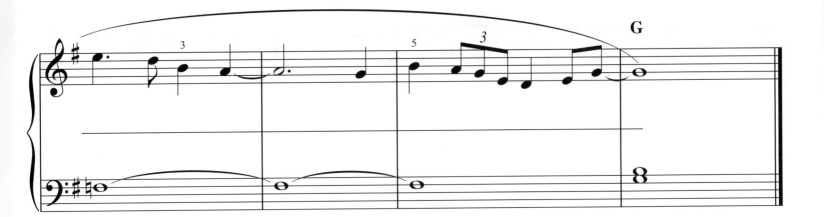

TRY EVERYTHING

from ZOOTOPIA

Words and Music by SIA FURLER,
TOR ERIK HERMANSEN and MIKKEL ERIKSEN

Moderate Dance beat

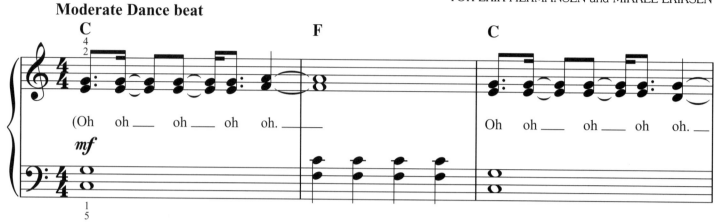

(Oh oh __ oh __ oh oh. __

Oh oh __ oh __ oh oh. __

Oh oh __ oh __ oh oh. __

Oh oh __ oh __ oh oh.) __ I messed up to - night. __ I lost an - oth-

er fight. Lost to my - self, but I'll __ just start a - gain. I keep fall - ing down; __

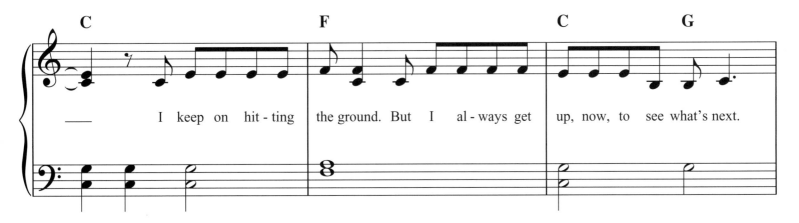

I keep on hit - ting the ground. But I al - ways get up, now, to see what's next.

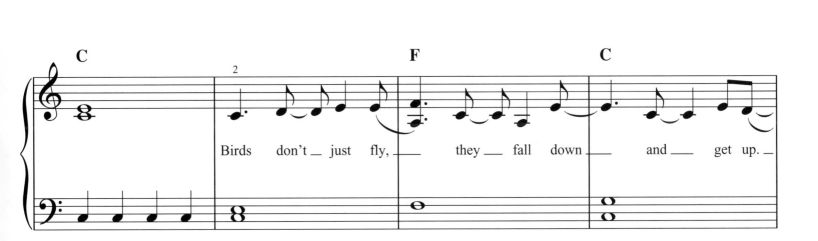

Birds don't __ just fly, ___ they __ fall down ___ and __ get up. __

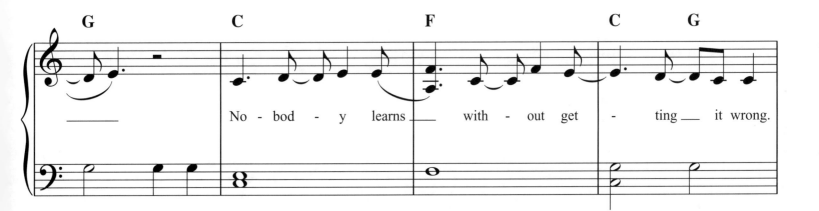

___ No - bod - y learns ___ with - out get - ting __ it wrong.

I won't give up; no, I won't give in ___ till I reach the __ end, __

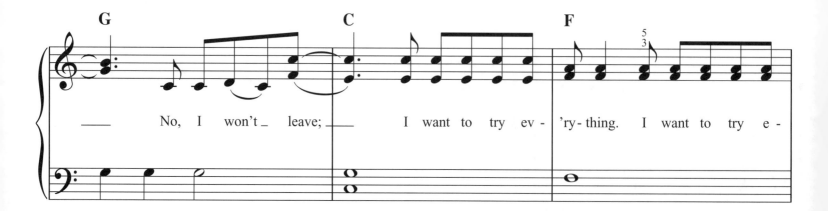

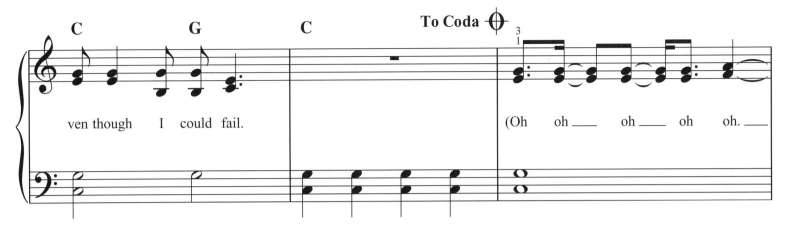

ven though I could fail.

(Oh oh____ oh____ oh oh.____

____ Try ev-'ry-thing.____ Oh oh____ oh____ oh oh.____ Try ev-'ry-thing.____

Oh oh____ oh____ oh oh.____ Try ev-'ry-thing.____ Oh oh____ oh____ oh oh.)____

____ Look how far you've come; you filled your heart with love. Ba-by, you've done

e - nough; take a deep breath. ___ Don't beat your - self up; no need to run

so fast. Some-times we come last, but we did our best. ___ I won't give

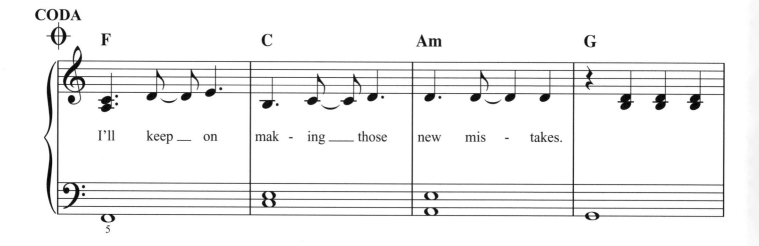

CODA

I'll keep ___ on mak - ing ___ those new mis - takes.

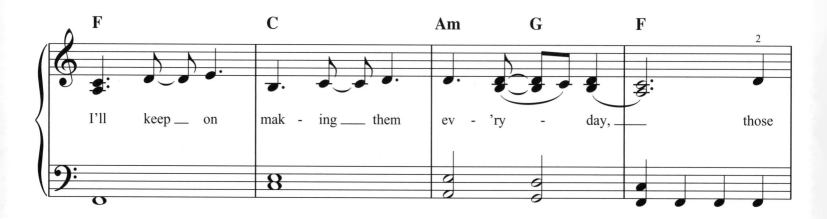

I'll keep ___ on mak - ing ___ them ev - 'ry - day, ___ those

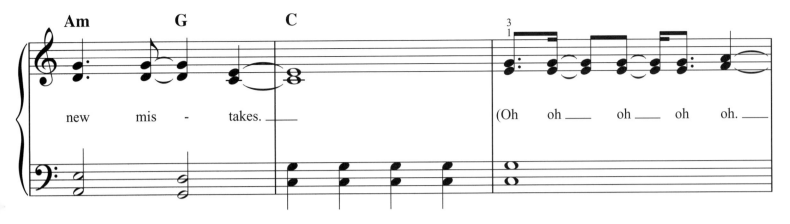

UNFORGETTABLE
from the Walt Disney/Pixar film FINDING DORY

Words and Music by
IRVING GORDON

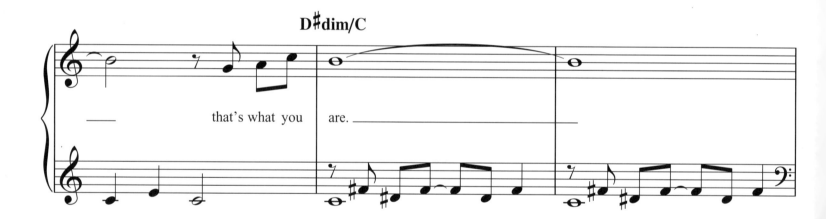

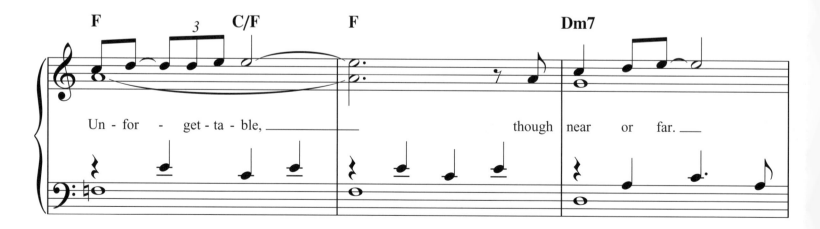

Like a song of love that clings to me,

how the thought of you does things ___ to me. ___ Nev-er be-

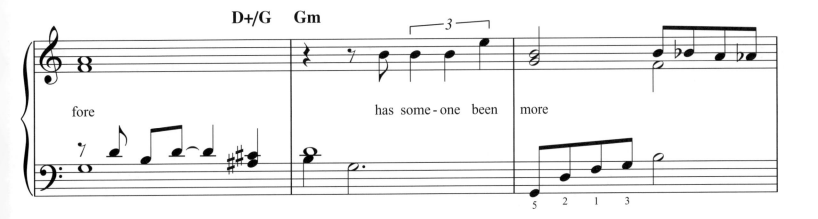

fore has some-one been more

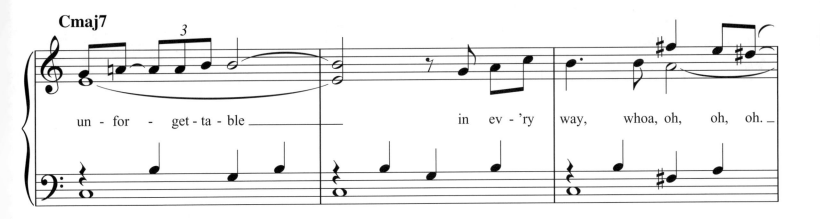

un - for - get - ta - ble ___ in ev-'ry way, whoa, oh, oh, oh. ___

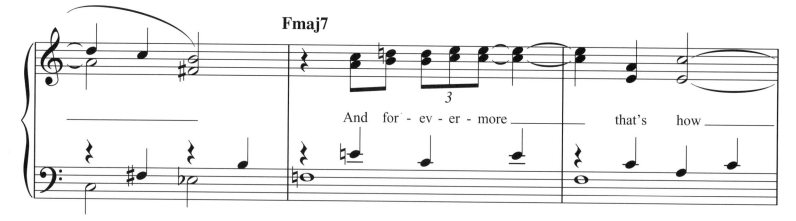

And for - ev - er - more _____ that's how _____

_____ we'll stay. _____ That's why, dar - ling,

it's in - cred - i - ble that some - one so un - for - get - ta - ble

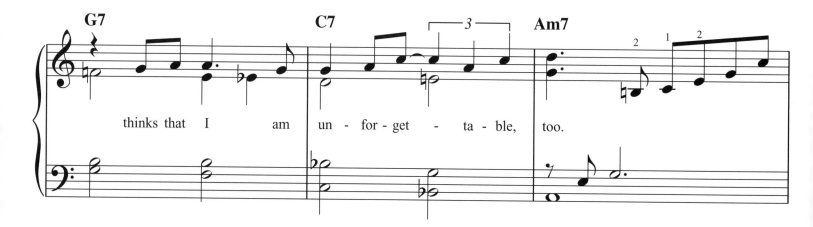

thinks that I am un - for - get - ta - ble, too.

That's why, dar - ling, it's in - cred - i - ble

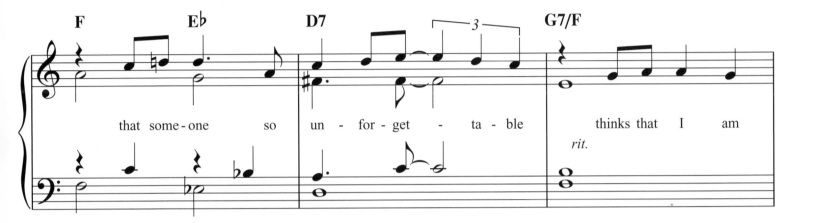

that some - one so un - for - get - ta - ble thinks that I am

rit.

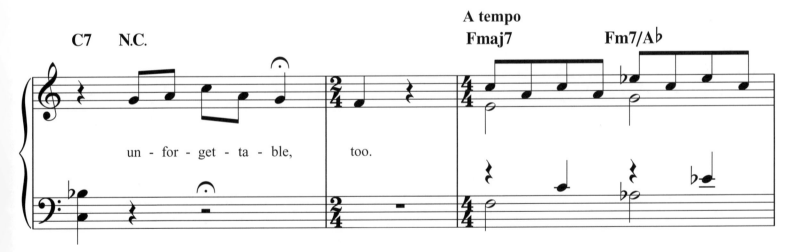

un - for - get - ta - ble, too.

A tempo

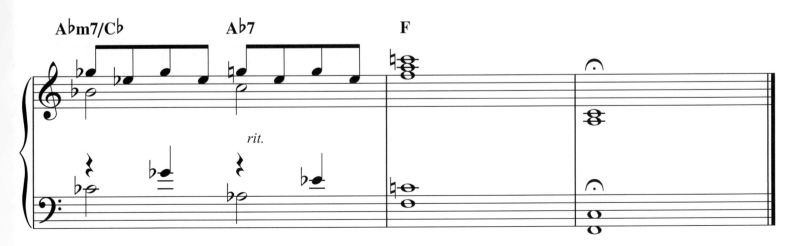

rit.

SOPHIE'S THEME

from THE BFG

By JOHN WILLIAMS

With innocence

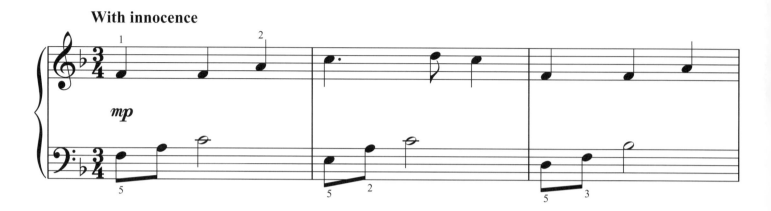

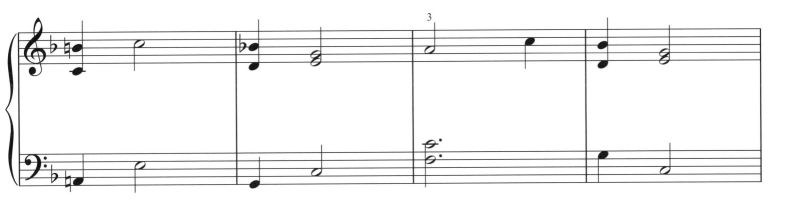

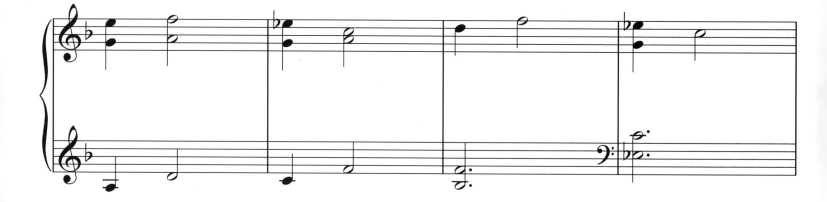

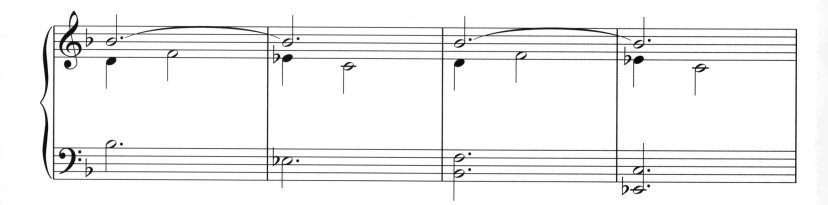

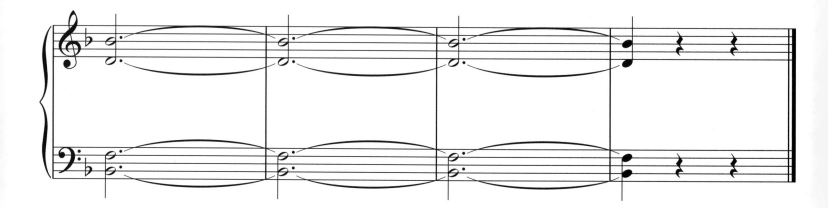